GARDEN OF A
Thousand Roses

SUSAN IRVINE

GARDEN OF A
Thousand Roses

How to Make a Rose Garden in Australia

HYLAND HOUSE

A garden really lives only insofar as it is an
expression of faith, the embodiment of a hope
and a song of praise.

Russell Page
The Education of a Gardener

TO MY VERY DEAR HUSBAND

This edition first published in Australia in 2003 by
Hyland House Publishing Pty Ltd
PO Box 122, Flemington
Victoria 3031

National Library of Australia
Cataloguing-in-publication data:

Irvine, Susan, 1928-.
Garden of a thousand roses: how to make a rose garden in Australia.

New ed.
Bibliography.
Includes index.
ISBN 1 86447 088 7.

1. Rose gardens – Australia. 2. Rose culture – Australia.
3. Roses – Varieties. I. Title.

635.9337340994

Illustrations after originals by Peggy Shaw
Edited by Vida Horn
Layout and Design by Rob Cowpe Design
Printed by Markono Print Media Pte Ltd, Singapore

CONTENTS

PREFACE

This book is the story of the making of a garden. I have not attempted to go into the very complicated history of the development of the rose. This has been done very often and very competently and would be out of place here. The reader wishing to understand something of this complex subject is referred to the incomparable rose books by Graham Stuart Thomas: *The Old Shrub Roses, Shrub Roses of Today* and *Climbing Roses Old and New*. The gardener looking for clear, faithful illustrations as well as scholarly text could not go past *Classic Roses* and *Twentieth Century Roses* by Peter Beales. These two authors form the nucleus of any collection of rose books.

There is often considerable disagreement among the experts concerning nomenclature, classification and, in particular, spelling. Depending on whether the third part of the name is considered to indicate a form, a subspecies or a variety, it may be printed in roman or italic typeface, with an upper or a lower case initial, enclosed by inverted commas or without. The simplest solution, it seems, is to choose one authority and at least be consistent in citation of names. The authority followed throughout this book is the great English rosarian Graham Stuart Thomas.

My warm thanks are due to Peggy Shaw for her delightful black and white watercolours; to Jenni Mather for her excellent colour photographs; to John Nieuwesteeg for his enthusiastic involvement in the search for and the propagating of the Alister Clark roses; to Ruth Rundle, Eve Murray, Maria Fawcett, Tid Alston and all the other gardeners who have so kindly opened their gardens to me and given so generously of rose cuttings; and to Vida Horn who spent many hours carefully reading the text and meticulously checking spelling of botanical names.

If this book conveys something of the joy in store for all those who turn seriously to the growing of roses it will have served its purpose.

CHAPTER

1

UNWANTED AND UNLOVED

t stood alone, the little bluestone cottage, unoccupied and unloved, by the side of the Calder Highway, which leads from Melbourne to Bendigo. I had passed it every week for five years and wondered idly who owned it and whether it was bluestone. It was so hidden behind thistles, blackberries and long grass that it was hard to tell.

And then one day there was an auction sign on the fence: 'Land for Sale'. Nothing about the house. The agent told me later that they took no account of the house. It was old and decrepit and fit only for the bulldozer.

I had driven past, but turned and went back. There was nobody there, but the doors were open. They could no longer be closed. And two sheep were standing in what I took to be the kitchen.

Four rooms only in the bluestone part of the house, two very tiny with irregular, sloping ceilings and low, wide-silled, multipaned windows. The walls, internal and external, were forty-five centimetres thick and there were big fireplaces in every room. The floors were sound, and on the walls and ceilings the old lining boards had never been painted. Two weatherboard rooms had been added later and here, too, the lining boards were in their original condition, mellowed to a rich mahogany colour. It was indescribably dark and dirty. The windows were broken and cobwebs hung from the ceilings. And I fell in love with it on the spot.

I went back to the auction sign and read it carefully. 'Land for Sale. Lot A 170 acres.' What on earth would I do with sixty-eight hectares – and me with no knowledge of farming and a very demanding job in the city? I resolved to put it out of my mind, banish it as a piece of romantic nonsense.

I did not pass by again for three weeks. I told myself to forget it. The auction would be over and the property sold. Probably a developer had bought it with plans to demolish the cottage.

But when I got there, the sign was still up – no 'Sold' sign pasted over it. I drove on to Castlemaine, where I had a weekender. It was charming and the garden was beginning to be very pretty. I had renovated the house – a quaint old cottage made of handmade bricks complete with cellar, and a dovecot in one corner of the garden which has since been classified by the National Trust. I had bought a pot of *Sternbergia lutea* on the way up from Melbourne and for half an hour I wandered round the garden trying to find a spot to plant it. There was no room left in the little garden. Clearly, I told myself, I needed more land. But not quite sixty-eight hectares.

The previous week I had spent half an hour in the Bookshop of Margareta Webber and had found, quite by chance, *Wild and Old Garden Roses* by Gordon Edwards, with 'Rosa Mundi' on the dust jacket, growing in the author's garden amongst a sea of foxgloves. I had taken it home and pored over it and decided that growing old roses would be the ideal occupation when I retired from my present position. So, of course, I needed more land.

On the way back on Sunday evening I called in again at the little stone cottage. It was a stormy evening and the wind howled through the branches of the huge old pine tree that stood just behind the house. The back door swung disconsolately on its hinges. The sheep had left the kitchen and were huddled in the tumble-down stable which had been built on to the front verandah. No one in his right mind, I told myself, would take on such a task.

But on Monday morning I rang the agent. No, it had not sold. It had been passed in at auction. If I liked to make an offer … I explained that I had no use for the sixty-eight hectares. Could I not buy it on four? No, that was not possible, but there was no problem. A local sheep farmer had been leasing the land for years and would be more than happy to continue to do so.

UNWANTED AND UNLOVED – BLEAK HOUSE WHEN I BOUGHT IT.

Still unconvinced, I made my offer. Too low, I thought, so that would be that. But that afternoon the agent rang back. The owners were happy to accept the offer and when could I come to Kyneton to sign the papers? I did so that very evening, and Bleak House became mine.

FURTHER ACQUAINTANCE

I thought of little else all that week. Since the house was unoccupied, I tried to arrange for early settlement. I drove up on Saturday morning filled with anticipation. It had been raining all the week and during the hour-long drive my windscreen-wipers had been working overtime. As I rounded the bend in the Highway and Bleak House came into sight I was filled with incredulity. Behind the house was a huge lake.

Now I knew I had acted hastily. I had not consulted my financial advisers (who would certainly have counselled against it). I had not had a builder look at it. I had not enquired about the carrying capacity of the land, or the quality of the underground water or the nature of the soil. But however hasty my decision, I was quite sure I had looked at it carefully enough to have seen a twenty-hectare lake if it had been there. And it definitely had not.

I drove slowly back to Kyneton and went to see the agent. He was apologetic. We should have told you, he said. It's terrible farming land. It floods like this every year, when the winter or spring rains come, and the water lies there for months. Hopeless grazing land.

Worse still, in his eyes, were the old quarries. There were three of them on the property, he said. They had been worked in the early days and the stone taken to Melbourne. Many of the big buildings in the city had been built of Malmsbury bluestone.

With a half-hearted attempt at encouragement, he spoke of historic interest. The cottage itself had been built of stone quarried on the place. But, sounding a note of gloom once more, the quarries were no use now – full of rabbits and snakes. His sympathy for me was patent, and possibly genuine. What would a city woman do with a property such as this?

I bought a pair of gumboots, a sandwich and a tin of gin and tonic and drove back to Bleak House in a state of mounting excitement.

The low carrying capacity of the land might be a matter of some concern to a farmer, but to me it was quite immaterial. But quarries and a lake were riches I had not dreamed of.

I slipped on my gumboots and started off down the paddock. The rain had stopped and the sun had come out. The hills along the skyline were a deep navy blue. And on the lake were black swans, dozens of them. As I got closer, a flock of mountain duck rose slowly into the air and wheeled away across the water in perfect formation.

On the far side of the lake an old road, hand-paved with stone, led up into the quarry. It was huge. Towering masses of stone, all covered with soft, grey-green moss and lichen. I found an old hand drill sticking in a block of stone and the remains of an old chimney. Had people lived, as well as worked here, I wondered.

A deep waterhole was overhung by elderberry bushes, and *Rosa canina*, the old Dog Rose, grew along its margins. Rabbits scuttled away from under my feet.

I skirted the lake and turned back towards the house along the southern boundary of the land. There was another quarry much closer to the house, quite a small one this time. It was shaped like an amphitheatre, huge slabs of stone forming a protective semicircle against the wind.

There and then I formed the notion of a quarry garden, remote, sheltered. I had a vision of it filled with daffodils, tulips, muscari. Rabbits don't eat bulbs. And neither do stock. The paddocks round Castlemaine, where the ruins of the early settlers' cottages were, are filled each year with masses of daffodils. Sheep graze there and rabbits in their thousands but the daffodils come back every spring. Iris, too. I remembered a day in late spring when we had come suddenly on an old ruin at Guildford surrounded by a sea of purple and white iris.

My quarry could be planted with bulbs. They are hardy. They like to be dry in summer and the quarry would be well-drained in winter. It could be fenced in from the sheep and the fences covered with rambling roses – little netting guards would give protection from the rabbits until the roses were high enough – 'Albertine', and 'Félicité et Perpétue', that dear little white rose with the soft pink buds that is to be found round so many of the old houses in this part of Victoria.

In a stone shaped like a giant armchair I sat and ate my sandwich. A misshapen old tree-violet (with a heavenly scent when in flower) overhung my seat, and a couple of magpies had nested in a self-sown hawthorn.

The birds were oblivious of my presence and I counted, in all, from my vantage point above the lake, sixty black swans. There was no house in sight. Only, across the other side of the lake, an old stone ruin and what is known in this part of the world as a shepherd's croft, long since deserted. The highway was far behind me and only the cry of the plovers broke the silence.

It was not just a bluestone cottage I had acquired, but a little piece of Paradise.

CHAPTER
3

RESTORATION

I was brought down to earth a week later when, at his insistence and with deep misgivings, I brought a friend up from Melbourne to inspect my purchase.

We arrived at dusk, and in the fading light the little cottage looked sad and forlorn. The back door shrieked a protest as we pushed it open, and a couple of bats brushed against my face. Inside it was dark, and John hit his head on the lintel of the door into the hall – people really were much shorter a century ago.

There was nothing to see in here, and we went out hastily. Surveying the sea of thistles from the back door, John tried to conceal his incredulity.

'Well' he said finally, 'sixty-eight hectares so close to a capital city has to increase in value.' No use to talk to a stockbroker of the scent of roses, of moss-covered stone, of wild birds and wetlands!

We talked of other things on the way back to Melbourne.

I had six weeks of holiday then, and resolved to spend them making the house habitable. Impossible to think about the garden until I could at least lock the front door, sleep comfortably at night and cook a meal at the end of a day's toil.

On my very first morning a large snake – I think he was a copperhead – slid away almost from under my feet just outside the back door. So the first priority was to clear away some of the undergrowth from around the house.

I went to see the farmer whose sheep were agisted on the land. 'Yes' he said with a smile, 'plenty of snakes there. The last tenant used to drape the dead ones over the front fence whenever there was any talk of finding a purchaser for the place. Puts people off, you see.'

I borrowed from him two large rams – large and stout with curling horns, which I regarded with some mistrust but preferred to copperheads. They stayed a fortnight and did a splendid job.

A builder came from Castlemaine, and we approached the question of renovations practically and systematically.

First, he insisted, I had to be able to lock it up.

'Right here on the highway … a woman on her own … the prison farm not a mile away …' (Youth Training Centre is, I think, the preferred euphemism.)

I insisted on restoration, not modernisation. I wanted, above all, to retain the atmosphere which had made me fall in love with the cottage in the first place. So no changes were to be made to the bluestone part. The two weatherboard rooms at the back had been built on later – about 1880, I discovered – and, with their steeply pitched roof, looked rather like a country schoolhouse. The very back room, I deduced from the broken remains of a wooden sink, must have been the kitchen. No stove – that had been purloined long ago. It had one small window only and, since the internal walls were the colour of old mahogany, it was difficult to see one's hand before one's face.

Ivan put in a whole wall of multipaned windows facing east, and another facing north, and high, narrow French doors opening south to a terrace.

Since I spend the least possible amount of time in the kitchen, I decided not to waste this room on such mundane things, and it became the dining room. The sun streamed in in the morning, and I could watch it set over Mount Alexander in the evening. And as the garden progressed in the years that followed, this room became a sheer joy and a vantage point from which to view the whole.

The inner weatherboard room became the kitchen. A huge skylight let in both sun and light. The floor was covered with deep blue ceramic tiles and a tiny room which had housed a tin bath (but had no water or taps!) became a walk-in pantry. A large Scottish slow-combustion stove (my birthday present to myself) ensured that this part of the house at least would always be warm.

All those practical and essential things such as power, plentiful hot water and a very pretty bathroom, were added in the next couple of months.

We had a small dispute about the handmade bricks which made the floor of the front verandah. They were uneven, and broken in places, and Ivan's builder's soul could not contemplate them with any degree of equanimity. They were a blot on his otherwise meticulously finished article. To me, they were in keeping with the shingles which were still to be seen on the verandah under the iron roof and belonged to the bluestone part of the cottage which we had resolved not to alter. They are still there today!

The four bluestone rooms were dark, with one window each and the roof coming down steeply over the verandah. It was difficult to see how this could be changed without altering the character of the whole. Finally, in an inspired moment, I thought of dormer windows in the roof constructed as light wells. We put in three, one for each of the front rooms and one for the central hall, and the inside was transformed. There was one clouded moment when we had a slight alteration with the Shire Engineer who insisted we were putting in upstairs rooms without a Council permit.

The internal walls in this part of the house, too, were old lining boards of the same deep, rich mahogany colour, but here they extended only to the traditional metre, and above that was wallpaper – old, grimy, the pattern no longer visible. I started to strip it and found another layer underneath, and another, and another, and underneath all that was hessian, stretched tight. I did the stripping myself, and, as the hessian came away, revealing the stone walls beneath, the dust of a century filled the cottage for days.

We replaced it with plaster, leaving the lining boards untouched, and I searched Melbourne for Victorian wallpaper. Big open fireplaces, sloping ceilings and windowsills forty centimetres deep lent character to these rooms. In a fit of extravagance I purchased an antique, four-poster bed.

BLEAK HOUSE WITH DORMER WINDOWS IN THE ROOF. THE SILVER BIRCHES AND THE HEDGE OF *R. RUGOSA* 'ALBA' ARE IN THE FOREGROUND.

With gardening out of the question until the builders were gone, and with my curiosity aroused, I read through the title-papers carefully to find out what I could about the previous owners of the cottage. 'The Hospital Farm' it was known as in the district. But its original name, given to it when it was built in the late 1850s, had been 'Bleak House'. I decided instantly to revert to the original name. I was very taken by the prospect of having a Dickensian flavour to my rose garden. Not that I really believed that Charles Dickens's novel had much to do with the naming of this little cottage in the Antipodes.

Bleak House was published in 1854 and it is just possible, since it was issued in serial form, that early copies had found their way to the young colony. But I think it much more probable that the property derived its name from the bitter winters, harsh frosts and howling winds that beset it for a large part of each year. I often thought subsequently, when sitting by the fireside and listening to that wind in the pine trees, that if it had not been called 'Bleak House' I would have named it 'Wuthering Heights'.

Seeking information about the original owners, I enquired of the Kyneton Historical Society who sent me to the curator of the Museum, which was housed in a fine old Georgian-styled building in Piper Street. Here I learned that the property had belonged to Sarah Ann and James Pennington, who had died at 'a great age' in 1872, she first and he only a few months later, 'probably of a broken heart' said the old lady in charge. Being childless, they had left the farm in perpetuity to the Kyneton Hospital. The Hospital had leased it out over the following one hundred years to a succession of tenant farmers until, in the last few years, with no power connected and no running water, it had been impossible to find a tenant. The Hospital had no money to spend on it, and when the vandals got to work, the decision was taken to sell it. That was where I had come in.

The good-natured curator could tell me no more, but suggested I contact the Kyneton *Guardian*. Here I found an extract from 3 May 1872:

> Mr James Pennington died in Piper St. He came to Victoria in 1839 and was a native of Tasmania and came to Kyneton with Mr. Thornblow, manager of Barfold Station, recently purchased by Sir George Arthur, Governor … James Pennington worked for him for many years. He did not believe in banks and hid money in out of the way places. Many expected that some day a large hoard would be found by someone. A roll of 50 or 60 notes – many rotted – stated to have been found by a surveyor's party out Barfold way in a roof of an old hut, was popularly believed to have been hidden by him.

Whatever 'hoard' had been concealed about Bleak House had been discovered long since. All I ever found was a halfpenny with Queen Victoria's head on it!

I was delighted with all this information and went from the *Guardian* office to the Kyneton cemetery. After some searching, I found the headstone – an unexpectedly large and pretentious one, obviously erected at some more recent date:

IN MEMORY OF

SARAH ANN PENNINGTON

DIED 10TH DECEMBER, 1871

AGED 52

ALSO JAMES PENNINGTON

DIED 5TH MAY, 1872

AGED 57 YEARS.

Nothing more. But I was greatly struck by the fact that these two persons who had died, to quote the Curator, at 'a great age' were much the same age as I was then!

In the weeks that followed I had a visit from a bookbinder. I was working in the front garden when the car drew up and a rather fine-looking man asked if he could possibly see the front room. 'You see,' he said, 'my father was born there and I have been so pleased to see the house being restored.'

I had a similar visit from a dear, old lady who told me she had spent holidays there with her grandparents who had farmed the property. Her first job each morning had been to draw two buckets of water from the well and take them into the kitchen to her grandmother. She was delighted to find the old well still there.

Truly we, who think we own things, are only caretakers for a while. I was reminded of a painting on a little house in the Black Forest which I had seen while studying in Germany years ago. I love their custom of painting landscapes and figures on the outside walls of their houses, and sometimes poems and homespun philosophy as well. I had stood in the road and learned this one and resolved to put it, one day, on a house of my own. And now, I felt, the time was ripe:

> Das Haus ist mein,
> Und doch nicht mein.
> Ich geh' hinaus
> Ein andrer kommt herein.
> Ach Gott!
> Wer wird der letzte sein?

Roughly translated it reads:

> This house is mine
> And yet not mine.
> I shall go
> Another will come.
> Oh god!
> Who'll be the last one?

It was not practical to paint it on a weatherboard wall, even less so on a stone one. So I had a plaque made by a local sign-writer who also wrote the poem on it.

I took it then to my friend Peggy Shaw, a very fine watercolourist. With it I took a copy of an illustration from a sixteenth century Book of Hours, depicting, of course, roses. She copied it faithfully and the plaque was hung on the south wall in the courtyard above a little garden which was later planted with paeonies and lavender, and a little golden rose which sprang up of itself, either from a seed brought by a bird, or from a root planted long ago by other hands. I do not know its name to this day.

THE FRONT GARDEN

With the builders finally gone and the painter due to start work, I sat down to plan the front garden.

It is tiny. With hundreds of hectares at their disposal, and a beautiful vista stretching away across paddocks to distant hills, with Mount Macedon off to the south and Mount Alexander to the north, the early settlers who had built this cottage had elected to build it facing due west, away from the view, and only seven metres from the front fence. So the area I had, in which to plan my front garden, was no bigger than the average suburban garden – and facing the Calder Highway.

It was bounded on one side by the drive and on the other – barely three metres from the edge of the verandah – by the fence which divided the house block (one could not dignify this jungle with the name of 'garden') from the sheep paddocks. On this fence were an old quince and a gnarled, old apple. I decided to leave them both. Height is important in a garden, and it would be several years before anything I might plant would attain it. And somehow they were a link with the past, with Sarah Ann Pennington and her husband, James, who had lived and worked here a hundred years ago and had made a garden. For there had once been a garden. All along the front fence, made of cyclone wire and in a sad state of disrepair, an old red Gallica rose was pushing through. It had bloomed, amid the thistles and the docks, in January, just after I had taken possession – a deep red old fellow, with a deep rich perfume to match.

And on the corner of the house, when the rams and the builders had done their worst, where no trace of a rose had been before, the purple rambler, 'Veilchenblau', had appeared. In the intervening months 'Veilchenblau' reached the top of the verandah posts. Truly the tenacity and recuperative powers of roses are something to marvel at.

And along the north wall of the house, under a tiny multipaned window, I found, when I started to dig, a narrow bed edged with bricks and in the following October clumps of Christmas lilies (*Lilium candidum*) appeared. They flourished against the protection of the bluestone wall and their heads nodded in at the little low window of my bedroom.

So here I had an area some seven metres by fifteen metres, facing west, with one quince and one apple on the left-hand fence, a red rose across the front and a deep purple one on the corner of the house.

It was essential that the garden be planned before the painter started. In the manner of old cottages the front door provided the only link between house and garden, so a colour scheme had to be chosen which would bring the two together.

The steep roof, coming down low over the verandah, was the dominant feature. So this was where planning had to begin. I do not much like red – either in the house or the garden – and green roofs do nothing for bluestone cottages. The prevailing impression was sombre – bluestone walls and the five dark old pine trees – so finally I decided on a soft, butter yellow, with that wonderful rose, 'Mermaid', climbing up the verandah posts, intertwined with a white wisteria. 'Mermaid' would have a struggle since she would get little sun – none until about 2 p.m. – but I thought that if any rose could succeed here, she would. Besides, she is almost evergreen and flowers throughout the summer.

With her single flowers she is often taken for an old rose and this would be in keeping with the old cottage. Actually, she was bred by the firm of Paul in England in 1917, a daughter of that rampant white climber *R. bracteata,* so vigorous that it has become almost a weed in some parts of America.

I needed a couple of trees to shade the front rooms from the westerly sun and decided on silver birches – their airy foliage, white trunks and autumn colour were what was needed as contrast to the solidity of the bluestone.

The front fence posed a problem. In a moment of false economy (since much regretted) I decided to leave it there and grew *R. wichuraiana,* the little white, ragged Memorial Rose of Japan, right along it, with a hedge of *R. rugosa* 'Alba'. Although it is a groundcover rose, I thought *R. wichuraiana* would also twine itself in and out of the cyclone wire – it might also do away with the necessity to weed under *R. rugosa* 'Alba', which is excessively prickly.

R. rugosa 'Alba' has been a wild success. The Rugosas must surely be among the best hedging plants. They grow happily to about two metres, are almost evergreeen, require little or no pruning and never get black spot or mildew. The single forms set brilliant hips, the size and colour of little tomatoes, and the foliage turns gold in late autumn.

Of *R. wichuraiana* I cannot speak so enthusiastically. It flourished. It rushed along the bed under the Rugosas and wound itself in and out of the cyclone wire. But it did not stop there. It takes root almost wherever it touches the ground, and it came up in the path and in the bed on the other side of it and set off across Council land towards the Calder Highway. Six years later I was still pulling it out and have resolved that the only place to plant it is on the wall of a dam. It would certainly prevent soil erosion and would be a splendid sight during its few brief' flowering weeks. But in a garden – NO.

With the frame set – the front hedge and the climbers along the verandah – and the two birches planted, I set to work to plan the rest. There was to be no lawn. Water would always be at a premium and there was, in any case, no room. A path must run, in true cottage garden style, from front gate to front door, and this I decided to edge with miniature roses – 'Green Ice' and 'Orange Cascade' (which is not orange at all, but a soft, warm yellow) because they are so hardy and so floriferous.

At the gate I had planted a forsythia, that herald of the spring, and later I sent to Tasmania for bulbs of chionodoxa, glory of the snow, which blooms at the same time – a deep gentian blue.

The beds were to be edged with muscari and *Narcissus bulbocodium,* with the cheerful little *Sternbergia lutea* and *Zephyranthes candida* for autumn colour. There were to be daffodils and the blue and yellow *Iris xiphium* and clumps of yellow day-lilies – in fact this whole garden was to be yellow, white and blue.

But there was the old red Gallica rose along the front fence. I decided, reluctantly, that he would have to go. Not altogether. I could plant him elsewhere, but he certainly had no place in my yellow, white and blue garden.

But I reckoned, as the saying goes, without my host. I enlisted masculine help and we dug him up – by the barrowful. I gave roots to all my friends, and then to all my acquaintance. Finally we thought we had eliminated him. Next spring, with the Rugosas all in place, up he came again, not in one or two places, but in ten. Six years later I conceded defeat. He is flowering happily in the midst of' the white Rugosas and his scent fills the whole garden.

Gallica roses planted on their own roots will do this. They form thickets, spread and multiply, and from every broken root comes a new shoot. 'Jenny Duval' (also known as 'Président de Sèze'), that lovely soft, pink-mauve, eighteenth-century rose of unknown origins, has done the same in another part of the garden, quite smothering the little pink and white 'Echo', and the early Tea 'Jean Ducher'. Ideal for large, rambling country gardens, but in a small garden Gallicas need to be planted as grafted plants.

The muscari make a carpet now under the Rugosa hedge, with snowflakes, which just appeared one spring. So, too, did an English gooseberry (more of Sarah Ann's legacy?) under the quince tree. It bears a heavy crop, and gooseberry jam is now an annual event. *Clematis montana* was planted to grow through the quince and a hybrid clematis, 'Fair Rosamund' (a pearly white), at the foot of the old apple.

Campanula poscharskyana forms a starry groundcover along the shaded verandah bed and masses of yellow and white violas, which seed themselves each year now, blanket the large, centre bed. The white ajuga is forming a dense cover under the silver birch, together with a soft, apricot-yellow violet, a gift from a friend.

In the centre bed is the double white Rugosa 'Souvenir de Philémon Cochet', the bright buttercup-yellow *R. foetida* syn. *R. lutea,* which came first to English gardens from Asia in the sixteenth century, and the white form of 'Cécile Brunner', the little Sweetheart Rose.

In the main it was carefully planned, my yellow, white and blue front garden, to bring a new spring, and sunshine, to the sombre old cottage. So with the plans made, I was ready for the painter. He came to see me one Sunday afternoon, ready to start the next day. I gave him a bloom of 'Mermaid'. That was to be the colour of the roof, the shutters on the front windows and the front door. Yes, he understood – and white woodwork on the verandah posts and window frames.

I drove up from Melbourne the following Saturday, filled with excitement and anticipation. As I rounded the bend I almost swerved off the road. There stood my cottage, its roof the colour of those raincoats children are urged to wear to make them visible at a great distance.

The painter was waiting for me, full of pride in his work.

'Johnny,' I said, 'that's not the colour of the rose I gave you!'

'No,' he agreed, looking slightly dashed. 'But, then,' cheering up visibly, 'it'll fade!'

It did. But it took six months.

CHAPTER
5

IRIS

It was 'Altissimo' that had first taken me, years earlier, to Kelsall Court on the outskirts of Castlemaine. There it was, clearly visible from the Highway, absolutely covering a three-metre trellis with its startling, velvety red single blooms.

I think it was my first acquaintance with a modern, single rose. Influenced, I suppose, by *Rosa canina*, the dear little dog rose, I had thought of single roses as being essentially early ones (I had still to discover the whole fascinating range of species roses) and here was this great flamboyant mass, three metres high and five metres long and bearing no resemblance at all to the deceptively delicate-looking pale pink rose that makes its appearance in paddocks and by roadsides and in my quarries.

I got out of the car to examine it more closely. It formed the boundary between the two enchanting little cottages, one brick and one weatherboard, which made up the whole of Kelsall Court.

And framed in the door of the weatherboard one stood Babs Mair. Stout, white-haired, with a face which fitted the description of Peggotty in *David Copperfield*, having cheeks so red the birds might peck them in preference to apples, a face alive with kindness and good humour. And on her feet were a pair of boots Gertrude Jekyll might have envied. She was one of the first great gardeners I came to know – 'great' in that she lived for her garden, and every green thing she touched lived and flourished.

'Yes,' she nodded. 'It's worth a visit. It's called 'Altissimo' and it's not an old rose at all. Fred and I saw it first a year or so ago and planted it to hide an ugly fence.'

They must have been among the first to grow it in this country for I found later that it had been bred in France in 1967.

Babs invited me in for coffee and to see her garden, and this was the first of many visits. In fact, Kelsall Court became a regular stopping place between Castlemaine and Malmsbury.

Babs and Fred were brother and sister. They had moved to the country and bought these two little miners' cottages long before miners' cottages became trendy. Each lived alone but they came together for dinner every evening. They shared an intense love of gardening, a taste for old cottages and for early Australian furniture.

The cottages were tiny. The weatherboard one belonged to Babs, its front verandah, cool and inviting, clad in ornamental grape (cut back hard every winter) and its front fence covered in wisteria.

In the low-ceilinged kitchen where we drank our coffee the wood stove was burning, chintz cushions were on the chairs, pots of geraniums stood in the window and the kettle sang. All that was missing from the Helen Allingham painting was the cat. I looked for him in vain. Babs was a bird-lover.

She and Fred had bought the cottages ten years ago in a very bad state of repair. There was no garden. They stood in a paddock surrounded by those unsightly mullock heaps which characterise old mining towns.

And in these unpromising surroundings they had created an oasis. Each time I called in we walked slowly round the garden to see what was in flower. It was the best course in horticulture I could possibly have had. From Babs I learnt about groundcovers. She gave me roots of *Campanula poscharskyana* and *Campanula porten-schlagiana*, and of the soft blue prostrate rosemary *Rosmarinus officinalis* 'Prostratus' which trailed down over the retaining wall at the back of the cottage and asks so little care. From Babs I learnt to cover fences, not only with roses but with clematis and jasmine and ornamental grape. Through Babs I came to know Gertrude Jekyll. She lent me that wonderful book *Colour Schemes for the Flower Garden* and the biography by Betty Massingham. Indeed there was much of that grand old gardener (apart from her boots) in Babs herself, in her intimate knowledge of every one of her plants, her generosity, and her total disregard of her ailing body – Babs was crippled with arthritis.

I visited them the week after I had bought Bleak House. Babs had seen it often as she passed up and down the Highway. She had given me so much help to create my little garden in Castlemaine, and I think she was secretly appalled at the thought of my exchanging it for this windswept expanse. However, she set about that very week striking pieces of ornamental grape and honeysuckle.

Fred's reaction was different. 'You will have room for the iris,' he cried with delight.

Years earlier, when he had owned that picturesque stone cottage which is now Badgers' Keep, Fred had dreamed of starting an iris nursery. He had imported high-quality stock from America and started out full of hope. Age and ill health had overtaken him and he had given them, some time since, to two green-fingered sisters who lived in an old sandstone cottage in Chewton. They, too, had found the task beyond them and Fred knew that they were now, in their turn, looking for a home for the iris.

The following Saturday – I was still working very hard in Melbourne and had only weekends for Bleak House and the garden – I found myself knocking on Margaret and Helen's front door, a door which opened straight off the footpath and gave no hint of the rambling garden behind, which sloped right down to the banks of Forest Creek, that scene of such frenzied activity during the gold rushes.

I received a very warm welcome. The sisters had planted the whole orchard with iris but the task of looking after them was quite beyond them. Margaret led me out through the tiny kitchen to see for myself.

There they were, in symmetrical beds, under gnarled old apple and pear trees and totally overgrown with weeds. Margaret was apologetic. 'Such beautiful iris,' she said, 'the most wonderful colours. But my back has gone and neither of us can garden any more'.

I arranged to collect them over the next few weeks and each Saturday saw me

'The Apothecary's Rose' with tall bearded iris.

'Maigold' in a mixed border of lupins (on the right), *Penstemon* 'White Swan', iris and scabiosa (courtesy *Your Garden*).

knocking on that door with a couple of large, green garbage bags, a spade and a fork. And each Saturday I received the same warm welcome – a cup of tea in the kitchen, homemade biscuits, a pot of jam, a jar of dried lavender.

Gradually the iris were moved to Bleak House. There was, of course, no garden there yet, but this was an opportunity not to be missed. So I borrowed a small rotary hoe and dug a strip along the fence. This would provide a temporary home. Their names had been lost long ago and, as they had not been planted in any kind of order, the colours were mixed.

After four or five Saturdays spent in this way I felt I had all the iris I could handle and broached the subject of payment. Margaret looked shocked and Helen, gentle, white-haired Helen, crept away in embarrassment. 'Oh, but we couldn't take *money* for them. We're just so pleased they've found another home.'

I brushed this aside. I spoke of business, of material needs which we all have, of being practical. All to no avail. I felt I had hurt their feelings. Finally, and very tentatively, Margaret mentioned that they *would* love a new carpet in the living room. So it was settled. Necessary phone calls were made and a few weeks later the new carpet, a soft, warm pink, was installed.

Iris are wonderful companions for roses. I am sure I did not know *how* wonderful when I collected them. They don't mind frost and heavy winter rains. They don't mind heat – in fact, they seem to love it. At Bleak House they are never watered. The roses are on a trickle line but there are no outlets for the iris, and they don't seem to mind. Like roses, they like the sun, and like roses they appreciate a handful of lime now and then (except for the water iris).

And they are quite unpalatable to rabbits. When I first planted them in their temporary home the fence consisted of a few old wooden posts and rusted strands of wire. The rabbit population was immense and growing daily (I decided they must all be Catholics).

Fred's iris were all of the tall, bearded variety. Over the years many other iris were added to the garden.

Through those bleak days of July and August when the roses, having been pruned, look as though there is no life in them, the little *Iris unguicularis* (which we used to call by the much simpler name 'stylosa') send forth a wealth of powder blue flowers. There is a white form, too, and a deeper mauve variegated form, but these are harder to come by.

Then in October, when, with the daffodils and narcissi over, the garden seems to hold its breath until the flowering of the Banksias heralds the onset of the rose season, the *Iris pumila* and *Iris innominata* are among the chief joys of the garden. Both come in a wide range of colours, multiply with astonishing speed and need dividing every three years or so.

And then, dignified and stately, come the tall, bearded iris, usually coinciding with the first roses. There were many soft yellow ones among Fred's collection. The yellow roses, which were the last to be introduced to our gardens (none of the species roses from Europe is yellow), are the first to bloom. I planted 'Frühlings-anfang' (Onset of Spring) and 'Frühlingsgold' (Spring Gold) and 'Maigold' as a group. They flower together and abundantly and the bushes spill over the path and intermingle. And with them I planted Fred's yellow iris, not in ones and twos but in dozens. It is one of the sunniest corners of the garden and brings back each spring happy memories of Fred who imported them and Margaret who nurtured them and handed them on.

OTHER PEOPLE'S GARDENS

he front garden had almost planned itself. Given the position of the house, the drive and the front fence, I had only a very small space to play with.

The rest of the 'garden' was quite another matter, consisting as it did of nothing but flat paddocks stretching away for what seemed a vast distance to north and east. No trees except for five old pines, planted, I suppose, as a nostalgic reminder of 'the old country' which was 'home' to the original settlers, and two of the biggest boobyallas (*Myoporum insulare*) I have ever seen, on the south side of the house. One of these blew down in a storm shortly after I moved in, and the other was so infirm that I was persuaded to have it cut down. The gardener who did the cutting left a stump some one and a half metres high. It is a gnarled old stump, and presents an Arthur Rackham-type face to the world – or rather to my back door, where it seemed to watch with derision all of my comings and goings. Over the next weeks I started to plan the garden.

Formal gardens are possible in Australia. Indeed, I think we must be the only gardeners in the world who think we have to make a choice between indigenous and 'exotic' plants. Some of us even go so far as to make it a moral issue, seeing it as a virtue to plant only 'natives' and totally ignoring the great wealth of plant material which botanists, travellers and naturalists have made available to us over the last two hundred years or so.

But the idea of a formal rose garden on the open plains of Central Victoria did seem incongruous. I had visited Cathlaw at New Gisborne the previous year during daffodil time when not only daffodils but also chionodoxa – regarded as a rarity by most Australian gardeners – formed a carpet under towering trees, predominantly oaks, for this is a garden with strong European connections, planned and planted by three women who made frequent trips to England and the Continent.

My most vivid and lasting impression of Cathlaw is of a small space on the east side of the house totally enclosed by a tall, dark cypress hedge at least three metres high. Within this enclosure was nothing but lawn, save for a small, formal pool, shaped like the ace of spades. Around the pool was a bed of brilliant scarlet geums

('Mrs Bradshaw'), startling, against the dark green of the cypress. I felt for a moment that I had stepped into Italy.

No hope of tall, dark cypress hedges on my open plains – they would take years to establish and I wanted results in a hurry! I had a suspicion that 'true' gardeners do not think like this, and I thought of Betty Ross-Watt at Cathlaw who came upon her mother one day aged ninety-four, planting a new tree. She was well aware that it would not flower for fourteen or fifteen years, but to her it was the creation of the garden that was important. Whether she would be there to see it in its maturity was irrelevant.

My mind turned, too, to Bolobek, that most formal and tranquil and restrained of Australian gardens. I thought of the formal little rose garden, surrounded on three sides by three-metre-high brick walls – mellow old bricks, kept when the original house was demolished – with pear trees espaliered against them and clematis growing through the pears. Rectangular beds and a sundial as a centre-piece, flanked by clipped box balls, little box hedges and *Alchemilla mollis* – a classic English rose garden. But it, too, was in the setting of an English garden, dominated by towering English trees over a century old.

I resolved to pay another visit to Tanglewood, my friend Maria Fawcett's garden at Donvale, not out of any desire to reproduce design, or plantings, or structures, but because it is a garden with which I feel a deep kinship. Both it and Cathlaw are very personal gardens, designed and worked by their owners and evolving over a long period. If you accept Russell Page's dictum that 'a garden really lives only insofar as it is an expression of faith, the embodiment of a hope and a song of praise', then your garden must be a personal creation.

Knowledge of plants will be acquired in many ways, design concepts influenced by many gardens and many gardeners, but if you are to create the sort of garden Russell Page was writing of, a great deal must come from within yourself.

Maria's garden is one such. It is the sort of garden we dream about, the Secret Garden of our childhood, an entirely personal creation yet a source of inspiration and refreshment of the spirit to many. 'You cannot give people happiness,' she said to me on my first visit, 'any more than you can give a bird song – but the garden can give something nothing else gives.'

Her garden covers about one hectare. It could be anywhere, for it is entirely screened from the outside world by tall trees, high fences, tangled hedges of camellias and roses and honeysuckle.

Little paths – not swept, not tidy – twist and turn through forests of camellias – the seedlings are allowed to grow where they will – huge crab-apples (not pruned or shaped) – *Malus* x 'Eleyi', with its deep plum-coloured leaves, in magnificent flower, with the grey foliage of wattles behind it and lilacs as a foreground. Helle-bores have seeded everywhere – no need to weed where they and the forget-me-nots have formed so thick a carpet. There is an old belief that hellebores afford protection from evil spirits, so they are planted at the back door, too.

At the end of the garden is a solid wall of the white Banksia rose, interspersed with *Rosa laevigata*, the 'Cherokee Rose'. Brought from China in 1759 it flowers early, as does the Banksia, and is covered in earliest spring with large, single white flowers with superb golden stamens. And growing through them both is a pink honeysuckle. The scent is intoxicating. The ring-tailed possums feast on the young buds – 'but it doesn't matter,' said Maria 'there is enough for all of us'.

The old roses, Gallicas, Albas and Damasks, have long ago outgrown their beds and form great banks. Many have been gifts from friends, so, struck from cuttings, have formed dense thickets. Many of them have no names. To Maria this is immaterial. Their beauty is not enhanced by their being ticketed and labelled.

A mysterious, deep red rose cascades down from the very top of an old apple tree – 'it's a Bach fugue,' said Maria, 'all intertwined'. It is 'Château de Clos Vougeot', described by Graham Stuart Thomas as 'containing all the oldest wine' and by Jack Harkness as 'the dark red rose of our dreams, the darkest red, black as night, to be stroked with the eyes, velvet and voluptuous …'

Bulbs grow everywhere. Sparaxis form a carpet at the side door, where they were never planted. A forest of Japanese anemones (*Anemone hupehensis*) is at the back door. Little paths, dotted with English daisies (*Bellis perennis*), lead through tall banks of shrubs. Dragons pop out from behind the leaves of the giant arum lily, 'Green Goddess', nymphs shelter under overhanging branches, Aladdin jars mark the turning point of a pathway. And everywhere there is the song of birds.

There are wonderful trees in the garden. I go each year in autumn especially to see the persimmon. There are species lilacs from China with most exquisite, pale pink, single blooms – valued not because they are rare, but because they are beautiful.

Rarities for their own sake hold no attraction for Maria, surrounded as she is by daily miracles. The little cherry plum trees are among her favourites, and the magical winter-flowering *Parrotia persica* whose tiny flowers glint in the sun like thousands of rubies. She would certainly say, with Walter de la Mare:

> The lovely in life is the familiar,
> And only the lovelier for continuing strange.

Maria shares her garden, not only with the birds, who are safe and valued here, but also with her Siamese cats (who seem not to be hunters) and even with a fox – and with the many friends who come, as I do, for refreshment of the spirit, a re-charging of batteries. It is a still world that she inhabits, a tranquil and a very beautiful one – far removed from the world of getting and spending, buying and selling, just outside her gates. I am reminded always of the inscription on the tombstone of the President of the Bird Protection Society:

He loved birds and green places and the wind on the heath, and saw the brightness of the skirts of God.

WINDBREAKS AND HEDGES

arden rooms, since Sissinghurst has become the Mecca of gardeners the world over, have become fashionable. In fact, I would hazard a guess that, among trendy gardeners (and I leave you to make your own definition of 'trendy gardeners'), their period of being 'in' is almost over and they are in danger of being regarded as a gardening cliché.

I had visited Sissinghurst at the age of twenty-one. Vita Sackville-West was in residence then, but it was as the author of *All Passion Spent* and *The Edwardians* that I saw her, not as one of the world's most creative, sensitive and inspired gardeners. Indeed, in my abysmal ignorance, I don't think I saw gardening as an art at all or even, such was the narrowness of my intellectual horizons, as an occupation to be taken in any way seriously, a gentle indulgence, perhaps, for one's extreme old age.

So it was with no thought of fashion that I designed the Bleak House garden as a series of rooms. Nor did I design it, as all good garden books advise, on paper and all at once. Rather it grew, section by section, the boundaries being pushed out as I felt I could handle a little bit more, or as I came upon a new group of roses or a new irresistible idea.

I had only one thought in mind when the first 'room' was designed: wind protection. For Malmsbury lies on that treeless expanse just north of Woodend over the Great Dividing Range, known to local inhabitants as 'Pleurisy Plains'.

The area to the north of the house, where I planned to plant my first old roses, was the first to receive attention. The sheep were put out and a two-metre-high fence erected for about a hundred and fifty metres along the Calder Highway frontage where the wind howled in from the west. It was made of treated pine boards, set about ten centimetres apart to allow the wind to pass through rather than its hitting a solid obstacle.

Then it had to be covered. I tried – after considerable thought – ornamental grape on the outside, with roses – 'Lamarque', 'Buff Beauty', 'Nevada' and 'Penelope' – on the inside. It was the least successful of my windbreaks. The grapes looked spectacular in autumn, but came through the fence and twined themselves all round the roses, making pruning a long and tedious job each winter and severely inhibiting the growth of the roses. 'Lamarque', which remains one of my favourite roses, hated the bitter frosts, which cut it back harshly each winter. In fact, the only really successful part of the whole arrangement was 'Buff Beauty', which continues to cover itself with glory each year.

Then I went on a trip to the north-east of Victoria. We were driving along a gravel road in the Buffalo River Valley when we came upon 'American Pillar'. I did not know its name then. I don't think I cared. There it was, a mountain of it, five metres high, dense clusters of lipstick-pink, single flowers, with a white eye, completely covering a little, ruined weatherboard cottage. In retrospect, I strongly suspect that it was the weight of 'American Pillar' that ruined it.

I took masses of cuttings, with no particular intent, and they all struck. It was as I was potting up the dozens of little rooted plants a couple of months later that I realised what a wonderful windbreak it would make – hardy (it had certainly had no attention in the Buffalo Valley), dense, quick-growing and impenetrable.

Wilhelm Kordes, the great German rose breeder, describes 'American Pillar' as being of 'a crude colour, lacking in feminine appeal!' And there is an entertaining passage in one of Vita Sackville-West's articles where she describes a neighbour as having planted roses right along his hundred-metre boundary fence. She was delighted until they flowered. It was 'American Pillar' and she described it as 'a long, angry, startling streak' which brought tears to her eyes out of 'regret that so fine an idea should not have been more fastidiously carried out'.

I resolved to be more fastidious. I do not dislike 'American Pillar' as she did, but a hundred metres of it along my north fence might be overdoing it somewhat. I had plenty of little plants of the purple rambler 'Veilchenblau' which had sprung up along the front verandah, and plenty of that dear little, very double white rose with the pale pink buds, 'Félicité et Perpétue,' which was to become one of my favourites. Named after two Carthaginian martyrs, it is almost evergreen, flowers prodigiously in early summer and flourishes in the windswept gardens of Wales and northern Scotland. I resolved to make a tapestry hedge of the three of them.

THE ENTRANCE TO THE ALISTER CLARK GARDEN: 'AMERICAN PILLAR' ON THE LEFT AND 'THE EDNA WALLING ROSE' ON THE RIGHT. THROUGH THE ARCHWAY A LITTLE GREY ARTEMISIA WAS USED AS A GROUNDCOVER.

We erected a cyclone wire frame, using bush poles instead of cut timber, and planted the roses about one and a half metres apart. In three years the support was no longer visible. The roses flower simultaneously and it is a joyous sight each December.

I had used rooted cuttings instead of grafted plants for the sake of economy – I needed so many. But I realised later that ramblers do extraordinarily well on their own roots. And there is no problem with suckers coming up from the rootstock. If they did, they would be virtually impossible to eradicate under that thick, thorny mass.

So successful was this as a windbreak that I tried another on the south fence, but there I planted the fence thickly with damsons first, as this possibly faces our worst wind. The ramblers grow all through the damsons and the rich blue fruit is a marvellous splash of unexpected colour in autumn long after the roses have finished. The common hawthorn, too, *Crataegus monogyna*, forms a good support for a rambler hedge, as do the little cherry plums which seed themselves so readily and flower so briefly in earliest spring. I never see them without thinking of the beautiful poem of John Shaw Neilson:

> It is the white Plum Tree
> Seven days fair
> As a bride goes combing
> Her joy of hair.

I find it difficult to believe that someone who wrote with such sensitivity about birds and flowers should have worked, for a great part of his life, as a labourer in stone quarries. He should, most certainly, have had a garden.

If I were planting such a hedge again I would probably, with greater experience and wider choice available to me, use 'Francis E. Lester' in place of 'American Pillar'. Like so many of our best roses, this was a chance seedling, probably from the Hybrid Musk rose 'Kathleen', and named after an American rosarian who rescued as many of the old roses as he could from the early settlements of the gold rush days in California. Very bushy and dense, it is literally covered, in early summer, with small, single roses in clusters, rather like apple blossom, and they have a scent which fills the garden (completely refuting the surprisingly commonly held misconception that the more petals a rose has, the stronger the scent). Later it sets little scarlet hips which hang in bunches well into winter.

I planted another section of the Calder Highway fence later, just with 'Albertine'. Certainly one of the loveliest of all ramblers, it covers itself with soft, salmon-pink blooms in late spring. Visitors often commented on the scent as soon as they came in the gate. I have a longstanding love affair with 'Albertine' and find myself putting in more cuttings every year with no particular purpose in mind. Bred in France in 1921, she will tolerate very harsh conditions – I planted my first one in a shaded corner not four metres from the trunk of one of the old pine trees. She flowered there as well as she did anywhere else and made a rather dreary corner a thing of beauty. Somehow, when the little cutting-grown plants are potted on, I always seem to find a spot where I could use another 'Albertine'.

The windbreak fences became for me the chief glory of Bleak House. They do their job. They have enclosed the garden and divided it into compartments. They have cut down the wind. For sheer prodigality of bloom there is nothing to equal them.

There is no need to prune these big ramblers. They could not flower more generously than they do. Unless they are getting out of control, pulling down their supports or taking up more space than has been allotted to them, they are best left alone to get on with it. If you do need to prune, it is best done straight after flowering as most of them flower on last year's wood.

We get little or no wind from the east and I did not want to block the fine view across the paddocks with a high fence. We had no need to provide a 'borrowed landscape' such as the designers advocate. We had our own.

So I resolved on hedges along the east side of the garden. Buoyed up by the success of *R. rugosa* 'Alba' along the front fence – it was into its second year and doing nicely – and seeking some semblance of uniformity, I decided to use another Rugosa here. I wanted a single one. The doubles are lovely but they set no fruit and these great scarlet hips are one of the joys of autumn. 'Fru Dagmar Hastrup', the pale pink single, has splendid hips, but she is probably the lowest growing of the Rugosas, too low to form an effective hedge in this sort of position. And so I decided on what is probably the most vigorous of them all, 'Scabrosa'. It is not my favourite colour – a deep, rose-magenta – but this is tempered by the contrast of the dense, cream-coloured stamens.

I planted twenty of them – and now have more than I can count. I planted grafted plants but the birds have carried the seed from those splendid big hips and they come up each year all over the garden. Some of the seedlings have come more or less true to type – we have had vast numbers of little 'Scabrosas' and little *R. rugosa* 'Alba's - but there are also a number of hybrids, some of them quite fine. One in particular, which from its position and its appearance I think is probably a cross between 'Scabrosa' and the deep purple 'Roseraie de l'Haÿ', I have become

'SCABROSA' MAKES A FINE HEDGE.

very fond of. It has flowered consistently for the last four or five years and grown into a fine bush, so fine that I am tempted to go through the necessary procedures and register it.

The Rugosas are among the hardiest of all roses. They seem impervious to wind. They do not object to frost. More than most roses, they tolerate wet feet. I have seen them growing happily in sandy soil at the seaside, lashed by salt-laden winds. They are grown successfully in the very shaded, damp gardens on the slopes of Mount Macedon. In Europe they are used extensively along motorways and in public parks where they receive very little attention.

They strike relatively easily from cuttings, but the problem of suckers then becomes almost insuperable, so that I would never grow them on their own roots except in a paddock or to cover a steep bank, or, with *Rosa wichuraiana*, round the walls of a dam.

A year or so after the planting of the 'Scabrosa' hedge a branch of the National Trust needed a quantity of roses as table decoration for a big function. It was late autumn and a quick walk round the garden convinced me that we had nothing in flower in sufficient quantitites. Finally I picked an armful of 'Scabrosa' hips. The Trust sent me a photograph later, showing those great scarlet berries in a silver bowl on a polished table. They looked superb.

There is an old, single paeony, whose name I do not know. It is exactly the colour of 'Scabrosa' and has the same rich creamy stamens. The two flower together at the very beginning of spring. The paeony is easily propagated from root cuttings. I took a few each year. It was my ambition to grow them all along as a border beneath the 'Scabrosa' hedge.

AN OLD SINGLE PAEONY.

CHAPTER
8

CLIMBING ROSES

had taken the advice of Edna Walling and 'defined my boundaries' – at least for this first part of the garden. As time went by
they were repeatedly pushed out as a little more of the paddock
was taken into the garden. But for this section, my fences were built,
my ramblers planted and my Rugosa hedge. Within these boundaries all I had
was a flat, bare rectangle of sheep paddock.

The first essential, it seemed to me, in a flat garden is height. In the corner
nearest the house, the south-west corner, was an old windmill which was at present
the only water supply. Beside it was a tank on a high stand and an old well. I had a
second high tank installed, as water was obviously always going to be a problem.
On the first of these tank-stands I planted the little creamy-yellow Banksia rose,
because it is the first to flower in spring, because I love the dense clusters of tiny
roses, because it is thornless and because, being virtually evergreen, it would hide
the ugly iron legs of the tank-stand the year round. On the other side of the same
stand I planted 'Wedding Day', the first of the many little white single roses I fell
in love with. It flowers much later than the Banksia, grows incredibly quickly and
covers the tank-stand in glory towards the middle of December. The flowers are
followed by clusters of tiny scarlet hips which hang on for months. And here, already,
was my first departure from my resolve to concentrate on old roses. 'Wedding Day'
was bred in 1950!

With these two I had most of the things I wanted for this prominent position,
but no scent. So on the second tank-stand I planted *Wisteria sinensis* and the creamy-
coloured climbing rose 'Devoniensis', known also, I expect because of its colour and
the texture of the petals, as the Magnolia Rose. This flowers simultaneously with the
wisteria and almost as early as the Banksia. Like many early Tea roses, it tends to
hang its head, so is best planted where one can look up to it and appreciate the rich,
full blooms. It has one of the strongest perfumes in the garden, and puts on another
lovely display in the autumn. I think this corner was one of the happiest combinations at Bleak House.

We built up the old stone wall around the well, covered the opening with wire
mesh to prevent children (or dogs) from falling in and round it we planted a tiny,

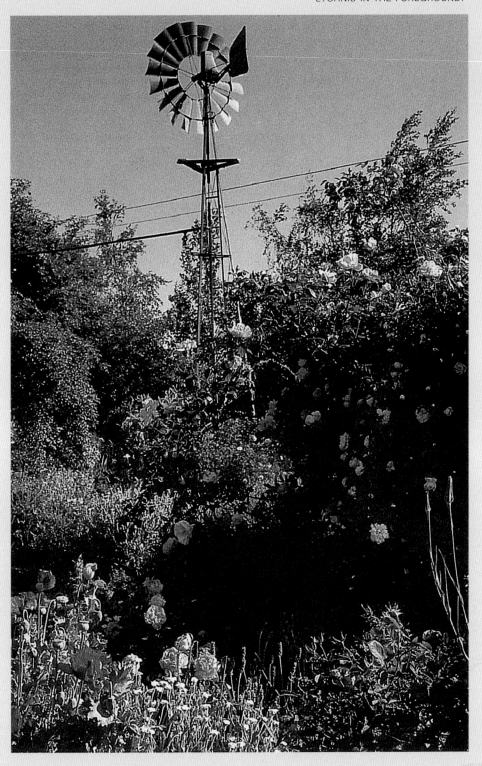

THE OLD WINDMILL WITH
CLIMBING 'MEG' AND WHITE
LYCHNIS IN THE FOREGROUND.

white double rose which I found growing vigorously in the Daylesford cemetery, and masses of pale yellow iris, with a few mid-blue ones to pick up the colour of the wisteria. On the base of the windmill itself I planted *Clematis montana*, resolving firmly to cut it back each year, before it became entangled with the head.

But all of this so desirable height was in the south-west corner. On the diagonally opposite north-east corner was a gate which led into the paddock. I resolved to take a path from the windmill to the gate with three pergolas built at intervals along it. Here would be support for more climbers.

Fortunately I did not want a straight path, for this is bluestone country and the stone is nowhere very far beneath the surface. So throughout the garden the shape of beds and the route of paths is determined by the position of the huge bluestone slabs, which are quite immovable.

I arranged with a local man to build the pergolas – simple, unpretentious structures, as befits a country garden. The first was something of a disaster. When I had bought Bleak House some of the verandah posts were rotted at the base and some were missing, so I had replaced them all. The old ones were turned and pretty and the builders had stacked them away in the barn for possible future use. They seemed perfect for this purpose.

The verandah roof was very low so the posts were short. I asked the old handy-

'ZÉPHIRINE DROUHIN' (LEFT) AND 'TITIAN' (RIGHT) COVER THE PERGOLA.

man doing the job to use six of them for the first pergola. 'But set them in concrete', I said, 'to give extra height, and strength to support the weight of the roses.'

When I returned next weekend there was the first pergola, beautifully constructed and already painted. The posts had been set in concrete, as requested, but *below* ground level. Even I, who am barely one metre sixty tall, had to bend my head to walk under. There was no way that Albert, who was doing the job, could walk through at all, he being something over one metre eighty, but he was quite content to go round!

The painting, too, was a mistake. The white woodwork was very effective for a few years, but by the time the paint needed renewing, the roses had grown so big that painting was impossible. I had to choose between cutting down the roses or leaving the pergolas unpainted. Of course I chose the latter, but later pergolas were built of treated pine and simply oiled.

On the first of these pergolas I planted what is, for many reasons, one of my favourite roses and one I could not possibly do without: the lovely 'Madame Alfred Carrière'. I have searched through every rose book I own in the hope of finding out who she was, this woman who had such a very lovely rose named for her, but I have found no mention of her. Her rose is almost white, with the most delicate pink blush. She blooms from spring to the end of autumn. She is richly scented and the foliage is lush and seems to suffer very little from any disease. She grows over six metres high on a wall at Sissinghurst, and Gertrude Jekyll grew her as a hedge, trained along wires. She is equally happy grown simply as a large, lax bush. She is excellent for picking and, best of all, she will continue to flower happily in semi-shaded conditions. My pergola was shaded almost until noon by the house and the huge old pine tree on its north-east corner. It worried 'Madame Alfred' not a jot!

With her, because the flowers are so exquisite and the associations so rich, I planted 'Souvenir de la Malmaison' – visions of the Empress Josephine and the garden she made round the hunting lodge she so loved – the English, so the story goes, even lifted their embargo on French ships during the Napoleonic wars to allow passage for those ships carrying roses for the garden at Malmaison. Inseparable from it, too, is the name of Pierre-Joseph Redouté, 'the Raphael of Flowers' who spent the greater part of his life painting Josephine's roses; and the Russian Grand Duke who, on his visit to Malmaison some years after Josephine's death, bestowed its name on the delicate pink, richly quartered rose he admired there.

But being transported to the Antipodes was not to her taste. She turned out to be one of the most vexatious, frustrating and infuriating roses in the garden. Like the little girl who had a little curl, when she is good she is superlatively good and when she is bad (which is every spring) she is horrid. The buds ball and turn brown at the slightest hint of rain or too much sudden heat (which, of course, in Victoria is our typical spring weather) and instead of being a thing of joy she is something we walk past quickly with heads averted, planning to return and cut off every hideous brown bud. But in the autumn, as if to make amends, she puts on the most glorious show, a profusion of palest pink, quartered, scented blooms which would soften the hardest heart. And so I continue to grow her.

On the second pergola I planted 'Albéric Barbier', which proved to be so rampant that a couple of years later we had to roof the pergola to give him adequate support. He puts on a perfectly breathtaking display of creamy-white blooms in early summer. The glossy green foliage is lovely all the year round. In his enthusiasm he climbed in no time to the top of the pergola, over the top and down the other side – a feat which few roses can achieve. Here he became entangled with the beautiful, salmon-pink single climber, 'Meg', which I had planted on the other side. When restrained, he set off instead across the lawn (a euphemism, this, for the paddock grasses we mowed, having insufficient water to maintain a lawn) and I earmarked him for future use as a groundcover. 'Meg' is another of the moderns who looks as if she must have been with us for decades. But romance is in her breeding. Released in England in 1954, she is thought to be one of the offspring of 'Madame Butterfly'.

On the third pergola I decided I must have something which would flower recurrently, so settled for 'Sea Foam', that most versatile of roses, equally happy as a climber (he climbs to the very top of a *Cornus kousa* on the front drive at Bolobek), a groundcover, pegged down to cover banks, or as a big sprawling shrub. The individual blooms are not striking, but he produces them with such generosity, great foaming trusses of them for months on end, and he would be a good foil for the lipstick-pink of 'Zéphirine Drouhin', which I wanted to plant on the other side. Thornless and recurrent flowering, the latter was nevertheless something of a disappointment. She is, like all the Bourbon roses, prone to black spot, but her main trouble was wet feet. The garden slopes almost imperceptibly towards this northeast corner and in our wet winters 'Zéphirine Drouhin' stood with her feet in water for months at a time, something no rose will tolerate. Laying drains in our great shelves of underground rock was a prospect not to be contemplated, but later we raised the bed a foot or so and she responded immediately.

A path must lead somewhere. This one led to the gate into the paddock. To give it added emphasis the path was widened to make a circle in front of the gate, from which other paths were to lead off. In the centre of this circle I placed a very large celadon jar as a focal point. In the jar and round its base I planted the tiny white groundcover rose 'Snow Carpet'. It lies flat to the ground, has diminutive glossy green leaves and tiny double white roses the size of a five cent piece.

So this part of my garden now had shape and form. To this point I had not needed to have recourse to the big rose nurseries or the commercial growers. I had decided to grow as many of my climbers as possible on their own roots.

Most climbers strike readily from cuttings which can be taken at almost any time of the year – in fact, whenever a kind friend offers them to you. I have found straight after Christmas a good time for these, as long as you water the pots religiously every day and give them some protection from the hot sun. In fact, Boxing Day cuttings of the big ramblers became something of a ritual.

Very fortunately for Victorian gardeners, there was a picturesque country nursery just outside Castlemaine which specialised in old roses, cottage garden plants and the older varieties of fruit trees. Centred round a four-roomed sandstone cottage built in the gold rush days, Badgers' Keep is surrounded by a true cottage garden: herbs, roses, perennials and fruit trees intermingled, with winding paths, stone walls and a chamomile lawn under a spreading mulberry tree. And it offered a wide selection of old roses grown from cuttings, as well as commercially produced grafted plants. The proprietors were true plantsmen (I wonder whether the feminists would insist on 'plantspersons'?) with an extensive knowledge gleaned over twenty years of running a nursery, a genuine love of plants and gardens and an unwavering insistence on correct nomenclature – all things often lacking in nurseries dedicated simply to profit.

It was from here that I bought all the climbers I needed for this part of the garden. They were healthy little plants, container-grown, and although they take a little while to catch up with the two-year-old, grafted plants available in many nurseries, the end result is immensely satisfying – strong, vigorous plants, and no suckers!

For the rest of the initial planting in this section of the garden I decided to use the grafted plants. Suckers are less of a problem under bushes than under ramblers, and I was still working in Melbourne and was not at Bleak House often enough to cosset too many little plants. This decision made, I sent away for catalogues to the big retail growers, Deane Ross in Adelaide and Roy Rumsey in Sydney.

CHAPTER *9*

THE FIRST ROSE ORDER

adame de Sancy de Parabère', 'Baronne Henriette de Snoy', 'Omar Khayyám', 'Tricolore de Flandre' – I delighted in their very names, exotic, evocative, conjuring up visions of distant places, other climes, other centuries.

'La Reine Victoria' – soft pink, fragrant cupped blooms named for a young Queen; there is 'Maiden's Blush', known in France as 'Cuisse de Nymphe'; and 'Rosa Mundi' (*Rosa gallica* 'Versicolor'), striped and seductive, introduced to our gardens in the sixteenth century and named after the lovely mistress of Henry II. Then there is the beautiful sport of 'Souvenir de la Malmaison' named 'Souvenir de St Anne's', found by Lady Ardilaun in the garden of her castle in Ireland and later cherished and propagated by Lady Moores. Pomp and ceremony enter with 'Cardinal de Richelieu', Minister to Louis XIII for eighteen years, a rich velvety purplish-red; and a hint of something sinister with 'Robert le Diable', a menacing figure in French history and legend. He achieved new fame as the 'hero' of Meyerbeer's spectacular opera which took Paris by storm in 1831. His rose is deep violet, cerise and crimson.

Where does one start with a bare paddock in Australia at one's disposal and such a wealth to choose from? One thing was certain: there would be no place in my garden for 'Frilly Dilly' or 'Sexy Rexy'!

I returned to the volume which had been the catalyst for all of this, Gordon Edwards's *Wild and Old Garden Roses*, and read it again from cover to cover. It is not a textbook. Much as I needed to do so, I learnt nothing of botany from its pages. But I put it down with the conviction that here was a man who had found a great love.

My catalogues arrived from Ross and from Rumsey, both growers who sell direct to the public rather than supplying retail nurseries. Both were informative but I needed fuller information than any catalogue can supply. I needed books. It was no use borrowing them from libraries. I needed to be able to refer to them constantly. I decided on a trip to the Bookshop of Margareta Webber, acknowledged then as Melbourne's leading source of garden books and owned by Neil Robertson, a knowledgeable and dedicated gardener.

From Neil I sought advice. He agreed that a good reference library is an essential, even for an expert gardener. For a novice such as I was, it was a *sine qua non*. And so was born another passion, one that tends to become an addiction and keeps one constantly poor.

I returned home that day with the three volumes of Graham Stuart Thomas, whose name is almost synonymous with old roses: *The Old Shrub Roses, Shrub Roses of Today* and *Climbing Roses Old and New*. In these volumes I found the accumulated knowledge of a lifetime, an intimate acquaintance with the roses themselves and expert advice on how to get the very best results from them. For many years Garden Adviser to the National Trust in England, Thomas has designed and advised on many great gardens, among them what is, perhaps, for rosarians the most inspiring of all, Mottisfont Abbey. Here, sheltered behind the high, mellow, old brick walls that enclose what was the monks' kitchen garden, Graham Stuart Thomas has designed a garden which is a veritable museum of roses. But I was not to see this until some years later.

These three volumes, the start of my garden library, have remained my bible, despite the fact that gloriously illustrated rose books have come on the market since and I certainly would not be without the English hybridist Peter Beales's *Classic Roses* and *Twentieth Century Roses*. For sheer practical commonsense local knowledge I bought Dr A. S. Thomas's *Growing Roses … in Australia*. The Foundation President of the National Rose Society of Australia, there is nothing he does not know about growing roses in our conditions, so very different from those of England. For good reading, I sought for but could not find Nancy Steen's *The Charm of Old Roses*. A New Zealander, she tells of her travels round New Zealand and her search for the roses planted there by the early settlers, especially the missionaries, and of her later travel in Europe and her attempts to identify the roses she had found. Knowing of my interest, a dear friend gave me her copy and it has a place of honour on my shelves.

Equipped with these, I sat down to pore over my catalogues. Before I could begin to fill in an order form I had to decide whether I was going to plant only old roses or a mixture of old and new. All my inclinations were towards the old roses. On analysis, I decided that this was not for purely sentimental or nostalgic reasons. I did not want a formal garden. I did not want roses and bare earth. What I wanted was roses as shrubs, big, generous, exuberant bushes which could hold their own with other shrubs in a border, which would be attractive as shrubs even when not in flower and would not be stiff, bare sticks for a good many months of each year. I wanted bulbs and perennials and groundcovers with my roses. I wanted hips in the autumn. I wanted scent. I wanted subtle colours. The orange and vermilion of some of the newer roses I could well do without. And all of these things pointed to old roses. So, for the time being, I passed over the pages in the catalogues devoted to modern roses.

It was at this point, while immersed in rose books and catalogues, that I came home one evening in Melbourne to find among my mail an envelope marked Shire of Kyneton. I pushed it aside – correspondence from the local council is rarely exciting. While preparing the dinner I returned to it and read, with total lack of interest, that the Shire was considering three possible sites for a new municipal tip, the present one having been exhausted. Obviously a routine communication to all ratepayers. There followed three Lot numbers. I dropped the letter into the wastepaper basket. Tips hold a singular lack of interest for me.

It was as I was putting the plates on the table that a terrible thought struck me.

Lot 256 was the Lot number of Bleak House. Frantically I retrieved the letter from the wastepaper basket, smoothed it out and read it again. There it was in black and white: Lot No 256. Perhaps I was mistaken about the Lot number of Bleak House. I ran upstairs, tipped all the contents of the Bleak House file on the floor and hunted feverishly for the Title documents.

There was no mistake. This was no routine communication to all ratepayers. Bleak House was under consideration as the possible site for the new tip. I felt sick, furious, indignant and tearful by turns. Could I, in this democratic country, be compelled to hand over, and for such an ignominious purpose, something which had already absorbed so many weeks and months of working and planning, and had already become such a great love, the object of my dreams? The letter spoke of compulsory acquisition and added reassuringly that owners would be compensated.

I reached for the telephone book and rang the Shire Secretary. Yes, he said, it was correct. The relevant authorities had inspected the land some time ago – without my knowledge, I interjected sharply. Yes, that had not then been considered necessary. They had reached the conclusion after inspection that it would be the perfect site for a tip – it was, of the three under consideration, the preferred site. The old quarries, you see, and the swamp – he called it 'swamp' with a note of contempt – that extensive area of wetland, home to the swans and the mountain duck and the plovers, which I had planned to develop as a safe haven for them. The land was useless, he added, hadn't been farmed successfully for years. And as for the house, it had been established beyond doubt when the Hospital put it on the market, that the house was fit only for the bulldozer.

Had he seen it recently, I asked. Well, no, not in the last twelve months or so, but he'd known the place for forty years, man and boy. And the tone of his voice implied that his knowledge would be far better founded than mine. And he was a Realist, which I clearly was not.

I spoke of the renovation of the house. Yes, well, a touch of paint couldn't remedy those defects. The only sensible solution would be to pull it down and start again.

I spoke of the garden. Nothing, he assured me, would grow on those plains. The soil was no good. There was inadequate water in summer and a deluge every winter. Besides, the place was overrun by rabbits. If I wanted to grow flowers (an unmistakably contemptuous note crept in here), why didn't I take the compensation offered and buy a little block in the Dandenongs?

I spoke of the beauty of the old quarries, and heard, without any possibility of mistake, a snort of incredulous laughter.

Had I been growing pigs instead of roses, I might have got somewhere. As it was, I was obviously wasting my time. From him I got the phone numbers of every member of the Kyneton Council.

Over the next week I rang each in turn. Most did not want to know about it. The site of the tip was obviously a matter of no importance to them. They simply wanted a decision made so that it could go ahead without delay. One or two were vaguely sympathetic but assured me that, much as they would like to help, it was really out of their hands.

My despair knew no bounds. I put away the rose books and catalogues and spent Saturday and Sunday walking over the quarries, picturing them full of abandoned cars, old tyres, household refuse, every kind of filth mankind seems to generate in such unlimited quantities.

A letter arrived from the Shire Secretary. There was no intention of taking the house. I could still live there if I wanted and there would be four hectares or so where I could grow flowers.

Marvellous, I thought. A rose garden overlooking a tip! The perfume of the roses vying with the stench from the tip for ascendancy.

And then I had a visit from a friend, a lawyer. He was sympathetic but carefully non-committal. After lunch we went for a walk over the paddocks, skirted the quarries, climbed through a fence and wandered down to the Campaspe River. The water was clear and shallow and the banks overhung with willows, home to nesting ducks. There are trout in the Campaspe and Bill was watching for rising fish, obviously with an eye to a quiet afternoon's fishing. I was filled with a deep despondency and found it difficult to enter into the spirit of the thing.

A few weeks later I had another letter from the Shire Secretary. It had been determined, he said, by the State Rivers and Water Authority that the site would be unsuitable, as the water from the swamp drained into the Campaspe River and flowed thence to Lake Eppalock which supplied drinking water to Bendigo. It had been decided, in consequence, to take the site adjoining the Kyneton Cemetery for the location of the new tip. He regretted any inconvenience I might have been caused.

It was never discussed between Bill and me and to this day I do not know how it came about. With a feeling of elation I picked up my rose catalogue again, took out a sheet of paper and started writing my first order.

FIRST CHOICES

he roses I ordered that first year are, for the most part, the ones I would order still if I were starting a new garden. Repeated readings of the books I had bought initially and increasingly frequent additions to my gardening library ensured that.

Among those I love best are the Gallicas, which have been in English gardens for centuries. To be sure, they bloom for only three or four weeks in the year, and for the rest of the time their bushes are not remarkable. But what a glorious flowering it is!

There are such subtle, mysterious colours, blendings of mauve, purple, dusky pink and grey. I would plant together 'Anaïs Ségales', 'Jenny Duval', 'Belle de Crécy', and 'Cardinal de Richelieu'. And I would use nepeta as a border rather than box which seemed too formal for a country garden. The soft mauve flowers and greyish foliage of the nepeta would set off to perfection the colours in the roses and, if cut back after the first flowering, it flowers again after the roses are over.

'Anaïs Ségales' I looked for in vain at first. Nancy Steen had found her growing in abundance near the early settlements in New Zealand, especially near the mission stations, often having survived a hundred years or so of total neglect. I found her finally, but too late to include in this planting.

It was schoolgirl memories of reading and re-reading *The Three Musketeers*, rather than any knowledge of French history, which ensured a place in the garden for 'Cardinal de Richelieu'; that, and his rich, dark purple colouring, described by Graham Stuart Thomas as resembling 'the bloom of a dark grape'. I planted him beside the grey-leaved *Pyrus salicifolia* with *Stachys lanata* syn. *S. byzantina* round his feet, and found him infinitely pleasing.

'Complicata', her large single pink blooms with their golden stamens borne on long, arching canes, needs space. Her origins are unknown, nor can I imagine where the name came from, for she is in appearance one of the least complicated of roses. If she is planted alone as a specimen shrub the effect is arresting.

I could not have a garden without 'Charles de Mills', rich, darkest red and so many-petalled. Like many of the Gallicas, if grown on his own roots he quickly

LEFT: THE FAMOUS OLD GALLICA ROSE 'CHARLES DE MILLS'.

BELOW: 'COMPLICATA' MAKES A LARGE SPRAWLING SHRUB.

forms a dense thicket. I have envied Nancy Steen her findings of roadside roses in New Zealand and thought that it was only in old cemeteries that we were likely to find such riches. But recently, driving along a country road near Woodend, I came upon a great thicket of 'Charles de Mills' in full flower, and not a house or a garden to be seen.

A rose of great antiquity, found originally in Europe and South-West Asia, *Rosa gallica officinalis*, the Apothecary's Rose, brings with it suggestions of walled monastery gardens. Its bright cherry-coloured blooms are borne in dense masses on bushes seldom more than a metre high. Used in medicine it certainly was, perhaps because it retains its scent so well. There are historical associations also, as it is believed to have been the Red Rose of Lancaster.

With it I planted its sport, one of the best loved of all old roses, 'Rosa Mundi'. Of the same cherry colour, it is striped with white and palest pink and is said to have received its name in honour of Rosamund, the lovely mistress of Henry II. Major Lawrence Johnston planted it as a hedge round the kitchen garden at Hidcote – an unforgettable sight.

Then to the Albas. No words can capture the delicious scent, or describe the loveliness of the delicate colouring of these roses, with their matt green foliage. Nor can any gardener ask for more vigorous or long-lived plants than these.

They came into our gardens long ago, and in most cases their origins and dates are unknown. I chose *R. alba* 'Maxima', the Great White Rose, and the pale pink 'Chloris', also known as 'Dew of the Morning'. And at their feet I planted the white form of *Helleborus orientalis* and a variegated ajuga *(Ajuga reptans* 'Variegata').

'Königin von Dänemarck' grows to two metres. Her delicate pink flowers and soft grey-green foliage look splendid against a stone wall. I planted her against the side of the house and each year for three years a diminutive pardalote came and built her nest in a little hole in the stone just behind her. With her I planted 'Félicité Parmentier' and the ivory-coloured 'Madame Legras de St Germain' and, of course, 'Great Maiden's Blush', which has been in English gardens since before the fifteenth century. And if you have visited Sissinghurst, you cannot see 'Madame Plantier' without remembering how she grows to the top of the old apple trees in the orchard there.

The Damasks quickly became favourites. Their very light green, fresh, young foliage is one of the earliest delights of spring. An eminent scientist of my acquaintance recently grubbed out all his Tea roses and replaced them with Damasks, because he is convinced that the flocks of cockatoos which beset our gardens in spring do not find the Damask foliage to their taste, whereas they appear to regard the young reddish foliage of the Teas as a gourmet's delight.

'Ispahan' I love. It is one of the first to flower and produces its soft pink, deliciously fragrant blooms over a long period. And it seemed to mind less than most the harsh conditions of the plains of Central Victoria. And 'Leda', the Painted Damask, with its pale pink blooms each outlined in crimson – best in the front of the border, as the bush seldom grows above a metre.

I included 'Kazanlik' (*R. damascena* 'Trigintipetala') for its history. It was grown in great quantities in Bulgaria for the making of attar of roses. I found it something of a disappointment. The bush is straggly and the pale pink roses not remarkable. I have never found time for the making of potpourri and, in any case, to me even the scent of 'Kazanlik' is surpassed by that of others. I think I would agree with Gordon Edwards who dismissed it with the blunt statement: 'It has no garden value'.

I could not agree with him, however, about 'Quatre Saisons' (*R. damascena bifera*) which, he said, produces 'very fragrant double flowers of poor quality' and 'qualifies as ancient history – pre-Roman – rather than as garden value'. Perhaps it is happier in our warmer climate, for I could nearly always find a flower on it from early summer to autumn – soft pink, simple, rather ragged flowers of great charm. I cannot speak so warmly of its sport, 'Quatre Saisons Blanc Mousseux', whose white flowers I found sparse and often discoloured, perhaps by the heat.

Despite its historical associations, I was disappointed, too, in *R. damascena* 'Versicolor', known as 'York and Lancaster'. I found it straggly and the pink and white flowers undistinguished and washed-out compared with those of 'Rosa Mundi'. Perhaps it is happier in England, or needs better conditions than I could give it. I saw a splendid bush of it at Hidcote.

'Hebe's Lip', I must confess, I ordered for the name alone. When my roses finally arrived and I unpacked them, I found 'Hebe's Lip' (or 'Rubrotincta', as Thomas now calls her) in a sad state. The scion had quite broken off from the understock. I was about to discard it, but on an impulse put the scion in as a cutting in the traditional mixture of three parts coarse sand to one part of wet peat moss. I watched it carefully for a few months. It did not turn black, but neither did it show any sign of making new roots. I pushed it to the back of the shelf in the glasshouse and, after a while, forgot about it. It was the following winter before I looked at it again and there, through the drainage holes at the bottom of the pot, protruded little white roots. I planted it out the following spring (fifteen months after its arrival) and it rewarded me a few months later with two little creamy-white

'REINE DES CENTFEUILLES' PLANTED AS A HEDGE WITH *DIGITALIS* X *MERTONENSIS*.

blooms edged in deep rose. Like a delicate child (or a sheep which has gone astray) it has received ever since very favoured treatment and has responded accordingly.

But the undoubted Queen of the Damasks is 'Madame Hardy'. Indeed she is regarded by many rosarians as the loveliest of all white roses. The flowers are a good size, very full, and pure white with a distinctive green button eye, and they are carried profusely on a shrub which easily attains a height of one and a half metres. I never see a bush of 'Madame Hardy' without thinking of the English rosarian Peter Beales, who said he would gladly exchange a whole field of 'Iceberg' for one bloom of 'Madame Hardy'.

Then there are the Centifolias – the Rose of a Hundred Petals, the Cabbage Rose, the Painter's Rose – great, gaunt, straggly, thorny bushes many of them, but such full, tightly packed, rich blooms, and such a fragrance!

Some of them, like the deep magenta-coloured 'Tour de Malakoff', which can grow to over two metres, really need some sort of support – a wall, or a tree, or a tripod – and he is certainly sturdy enough to have a clematis growing through him. And some of them, like the adorable 'de Meaux' and 'Petite de Hollande' are almost miniatures – suitable for growing in a container. *R. centifolia* 'Variegata', with the charming popular name of 'Village Maid', is one of the loveliest of the variegated roses – softest pink and white irregular stripes, and the flowers borne in great clusters on long arching branches which really do need to be shortened back in July if they are not to trail on the ground with the weight of the flowers.

And a place of honour must surely be reserved for 'Fantin-Latour', that mystery rose who came from we know not where. Suffice it to say that it is aptly named for the great French painter, for it is the very epitome of romance.

And here I thought I should stop in that my first year. The Mosses and early Tea roses, the Hybrid Perpetuals and Hybrid Musks would have to wait for another twelve months. For I was still working full-time in Melbourne with only weekends and occasional holidays to devote to my garden, and it would take every bit of time I had to transform my sheep paddock into prepared beds before the roses arrived in mid-winter.

CHAPTER
11

PRELIMINARIES

There was much to be done before the roses arrived in June. I had read enough to know that my virgin soil had to be deeply dug, and manure added (if available), in plenty of time for it to break down before planting time. So I enlisted the help of Albert, the old fellow who had built the pergolas, and we set to work.

Across the bottom of the garden, the north boundary, was a huge pile of rocks. They were big rocks, too big for Albert and me to move. The ground everywhere was full of stone and I suppose that, years ago, this paddock had once been ploughed and the stones put in a heap, as they were thrown up, to be out of the way.

They were very much in our way now, and posed a problem. In the end we decided they would have to stay there but we would move those we could and form them into a raised rock garden. This we did over the next couple of weekends and were tolerably pleased with our efforts.

But this was not the whole situation. The rocks were so big that we had pockets fifty to sixty centimeters deep which would have to be filled with soil.

With a touching faith in the local suppliers and a total ignorance of the varying types of topsoil, I ordered a load from a local landscape supplier. It rained the day it was delivered and then followed three very hot days. It was heavy black soil and, by the time we came to work it the following Saturday, it had set like concrete. So this was not the answer. There had to be a better way.

My mind went back to Cathlaw. On my first visit there, as Betty Ross-Watt showed me round the garden, I had remarked on the many very pretty ponds. She had laughed. 'Yes,' she said, 'my mother was the garden designer and she was always making new beds. It was too expensive to buy topsoil so whenever we wanted more we just dug a new pond!'

Here was our solution. So Albert and I set to work and dug our first pond in the middle of our rock garden. We dug it as deep as we could. Then we selected the flattest pieces of stone and lined it, setting the stone in concrete to which we added a waterproofing compound and some dark grey colouring matter.

I wanted a rose to grow round the pond so I added to my initial rose order two plants of the Rugosa groundcover rose, *R.* 'Paulii'. It grows horizontally and is prodigiously prickly, which makes training it something of an ordeal. But it bears a mass of very pretty, pure white, single flowers with golden stamens. Unfortunately it is one of the few Rugosas which does not flower recurrently, but the foliage is handsome and it is as hardy as all its relations and I was delighted with it. At the back of the pond against the fence I planted several clumps of lad's love (*Artemisia abrotanum*); its grey-green foliage made a good foil for the white roses and it is hardy enough to need very little attention beyond a hard cut back each year.

Then I made the most terrible mistake – one I paid for dearly for years to follow. I hired a fellow with a rotary hoe and got him to dig my beds for me. He did a splendid job, digging deep and thoroughly and exercising exemplary restraint when his hoe struck rock.

But country gardens are full of weed. My most prevalent ones were bindweed (for which I came to harbour the most intense hatred), twitch – a near relative of couch, docks and sorrel. Every piece of every one of them cut up by the rotary hoe took root and flourished. I had committed the elementary mistake of not poisoning the weeds first.

I attacked them, too late, with the gardener's best friend and indispensable ally,

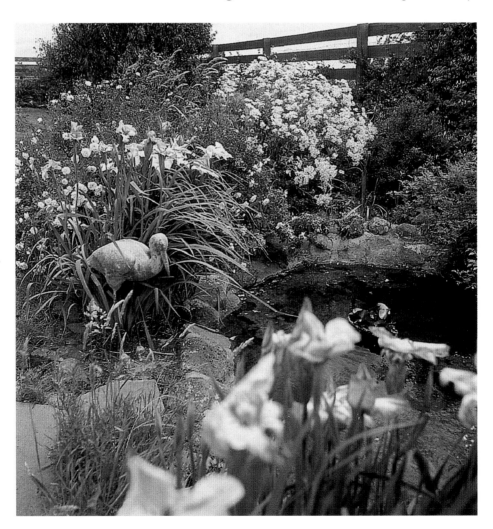

OUR FIRST POND WITH *IRIS ENSATA*. THE WHITE ROSE IS 'SWANY'.

Round-up, which acts through the chlorophyll in the foliage and leaves no residual poison in the soil. I do not like using poisons. In fact, I hate it, but after a year or so of painstaking hand-weeding I decided to compromise and bought my first five litres of Round-up. It worked well on the sorrel and I discovered that sorrel is also somewhat discouraged by generous applications of lime. Round-up works less well on well-established docks, which I concluded really have to be weeded out. It appears to work well on couch and bindweed but these are so deep-rooted that over and over again I found, just as I dared to hope they were gone, they would emerge triumphantly once again. I came upon a marvellous little book at this time called *The Labours of Forty-eight Years of William Lawson*, published in London in 1618. It contained, amongst other pearls of wisdom, the following:

> The Gardner had not need be an idle or lazie lubber, for so your Orchard will not prosper. There will ever be something to doe. Weeds are alwaise growing.

Here was the voice of experience!

Hand-weeding and deep mulching became a routine. I started with a magnificent supply of old cow manure. The hospital's last tenant at Bleak House before it became uninhabitable was a farmer who had conducted a Jersey stud. There was an old tumbledown barn across from the house and in this, so I was reliably informed, he had housed his bulls. I concluded he must have been a 'lazie lubber' for he had never bothered to clean out his barn and by the time he left the property, discouraged understandably by the lack of water and power and the dilapidated state of the fences, the manure was over a metre deep.

The builders had shaken their heads at the sight of it, condemned the barn as beyond repair and suggested putting a match to the whole thing. This suggestion I had firmly repudiated, for this was to me a treasure richer than gold.

Painstakingly Albert and I barrowed it on to the beds. It took many weekends, for the barn was a good size. Indeed I did not reach the end of it for over two years. But it gave the roses a wonderful start.

One other thing I wanted to do before the roses came was to plant a few trees. Not many, for roses like an open sunny position – they must have at least four or five hours of sun each day – and I could not afford to plant trees which might, in time, grow huge and block the sun. But I wanted a group on the western corner – no one really wants our harsh western sun – and I wanted to screen out the Calder Highway as much as possible. The five big pine trees which were there when I bought the property were all on the south and east sides of the house. To the north, where the main rose garden was to be, there was only one aged misshapen willow, broken and battered by a century of storms. I engaged a local treelopper (I'm sure he would not have laid claim to the title of 'tree-surgeon') with the colourful name of Paddy McGuinness, to cut out the dead wood and restore it to some semblance of symmetry. Paddy turned out to be just as his name suggested. Cheerful and charming, he hacked away with a will and my poor old willow was in no time reduced to a forlorn-looking, three-metre-high stump. In Paddy's defence I must add that within twelve months it had shot and grown prodigiously and no longer had any real need of the evergreen climber *Rosa × fortuniana* which I had planted hastily to hide its nakedness.

To link this part of the garden with the adjoining front garden I bought (being always impatient) two advanced silver birches (*Betula pendula*). These I planted in the corner near the windmill. A couple of weeks later I bought a potted rose from a local nursery and in the pot were six diminutive self-sown birch seedlings. Rather than throw them away, I planted them – straight into the ground – in the vicinity of the two advanced trees. If even one survived, I thought, it would form an attractive little group. All six survived and flourished mightily. Within eighteen months they had overtaken the advanced trees and it became a delightful little copse.

Influenced by Maria, I planted, in the western corner, two *Parrotia persica* and in this corner also two golden ashes (*Fraxinus excelsior* 'Aurea'). Then, as a specimen tree, and in memory of very happy student days in Germany, I planted a linden (*Tilia × europaea*). It did not like our hot, dry summers and made deplorably slow progress.

I had been given, the Christmas before, by a dear friend and valued colleague three lemon-scented gums (*Eucalyptus citriodora*). The accompanying card read: 'You have educated my three daughters. Please plant these in the new garden and call them Mary, Elizabeth and Catherine.' I was delighted. It is, I think, my favourite among the eucalypts. The avenue of them which leads from the gate to the house at Cruden Farm outside Melbourne must be one of the loveliest entries to any Australian property.

I had misgivings about them in our climate, but planted them and hoped. My misgivings proved justified for they did not survive our first severe frosts. I planted three crab-apples in their place – *Malus ioensis* 'Plena', *Malus* 'Gorgeous' and the bronze-leaved *Malus* 'Lemoinei'. These grew better than any other trees I planted and gave blossom in spring, fruit in summer and glorious colour in autumn. They happily tolerated our wet, cold winters and the hot, dry summers – and, an added bonus, they belong to the Rosaceae family.

CHAPTER
12

LITTLE PORTION

mall things have a particular appeal, and small plants tend to get lost in a large garden. I wanted, somewhere in the broad expanse of hectares I had acquired, a miniature garden – somewhere for miniature roses, tiny bulbs (crocus, species tulips, miniature narcissi) and for English primroses and auriculas which needed the sheltered, semi-shaded conditions I could at present certainly not provide.

And so I set about planning my Miniature Garden. It would have to be enclosed, both for aesthetic reasons and to break the force of the winds which howl across the plains of the Central Highlands. How to achieve this quickly was the problem.

Some weeks earlier I had decided, one still, sunny afternoon, to walk round the entire perimeter of my sixty-eight hectares. There was a narrow frontage to the Malmsbury East Road, which runs parallel to the Calder Highway from Malmsbury to Kyneton. Here, adjoining my land, I had found an old stone ruin which had once been a substantial home. And beside it, still intact, the shepherd's croft I had glimpsed from the quarry on that first afternoon. Made of bluestone with a shingled roof, it consisted of two rooms only, one door and three windows and a tiny corner fireplace. It measured in all six metres by four. Here was the perfect centrepiece for my miniature garden but there were problems: firstly, it did not belong to me, and secondly, it was a full twenty minutes' walk from the house. Out of the question.

The more I thought about it, the more perfect it seemed. Such a building would give the atmosphere I needed at one stroke. I had the bluestone. The old quarries were full of it. Cut pieces in all sizes, just as they had been chipped from the big blocks a hundred years ago. And I had heard of an English stonemason near Castlemaine. Perhaps he might agree to undertake the building of a replica.

Vic not only agreed. He was positively enthusiastic. So we measured the little building and made rough drawings. He brought his front-end loader and we started collecting stone.

Doors and windows posed a problem. New ones would be entirely out of place. Old ones, the size we wanted, were not easy to come by.

It was at this stage that I made a trip one morning to Castlemaine. On the

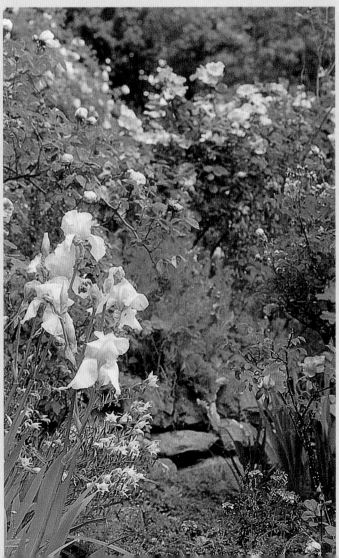

ABOVE: LITTLE PORTION WITH 'SWANY' IN THE FOREGROUND.

RIGHT: 'SPARRIESHOOP' AND IRIS IN THE FRONT GARDEN.

outskirts of the town I had to pass a little old miner's cottage, the sort that abounded in this area and around Maldon in the early mining days. It was entirely unspoiled, even to its picket fence and iron lace and the huge old oak tree that overhung the verandah. The renovators had passed it by. I tried to buy it once from the whitehaired old fellow who owned it, but he had simply shaken his head and asked, 'And where would I live then?'

I had watched it ever since in my goings and comings, and my friend Ian Hargrave, a painter who specialised in painting watercolours of the old buildings in the area, had painted it for me. I have the painting still.

On this day as I looked across, I saw, to my dismay and consternation, workmen throwing down sheets of iron from the roof. I braked sharply, turned, and drove back. It was being demolished to make way for four 'cluster houses'. Another link with Castlemaine's early history was gone. As I turned away I noticed the windows stacked near the gate.

'What are you doing with those?' I asked. 'To the tip, love,' said the workman in charge. And so I bought, for $10 each, three little windows, the front and the back door and, on an impulse, the old slate front doorstep, worn with the footsteps of a hundred years.

A month or so later our little stone cottage was complete and stood, isolated and exposed, in the middle of what was still no more than a paddock. An unwonted heavy snowfall a week later made it look, as a friend told me, like something straight out of Siberia. I worried then about the effect of snow on the garden, but soon discovered that its thick, soft blanket does a great deal less damage than frost.

By the following spring an area behind the cottage had been enclosed by high lattice fencing and work on the garden began.

In the back corner we built, with the stone left over from the cottage, a corner seat which I planted thickly with thyme. Lost in contemplation of the spicy scent which would be released by sitting on thyme, I quite overlooked the fact that the bees like it too.

The rest of the stone was used to form edges for the raised beds, built formally round a square, all the paths being paved with old, handmade bricks. A pretty old wooden garden seat made a warm, sheltered spot just outside the back door. It later became a favourite venue for predinner Scotch.

Water was still a problem, so we put a tank at the back of the cottage to catch the run-off from its roof. We painted it olive green, bound wire netting tightly round it and planted the pink, single rose 'Sparrieshoop' to cover it. 'Sparrieshoop' – the name comes from the north German town where the Kordes family have bred so many of their famous roses, roses which do exceptionally well for us here in Victoria – perhaps because they have been bred in a climate not unlike our own, with hot summers and very cold winters. Like 'Mermaid', 'Sparrieshoop' looks like an old rose although it was released in 1953. Unlike the old, single species roses though, it flowers throughout the summer.

I have to confess to a liking for good garden sculpture and used, as a centrepiece for my Miniature Garden, a slender, ascetic-looking madonna, work of the well-known sculptor Hans Knorr, originally from Bavaria. I had bought it some years earlier when he had owned a gallery at Emerald in the Dandenongs.

Miniature roses lend themselves to formality so I resolved to try a miniature form of posts and chains. The posts were barely a metre high and about two metres apart. To climb along the chains I selected the miniature climbers 'Candy Cane' (single, lipstick-pink), 'Climbing Jackie' (white), 'Red Cascade' and 'Baby Jayne' with mauve-pink double flowers like the patterns on old muslins.

Miniatures make excellent standards, so I planted standard 'Mary Marshall' and 'The Fairy' in big tubs beside my garden seat. The climbing form of 'Cécile Brunner' was put either side of an arch at the end of the garden. Although certainly not a miniature, its tiny flowers were right in this context, and it is more than capable of attaining the required height. For the same reasons, the first of the Noisette roses, 'Champney's Pink Cluster', was chosen to cover an archway over the front door.

The roses for the beds (which had been raised up to ensure adequate drainage in our very wet winters) were chosen with two things in mind. I had decided on a basically pink and white colour scheme, soft against the grey stone of the walls. And I wanted roses which would look at home in what was essentially an old rose garden.

Rosa chinensis 'M*inima*' was a must. Miniature roses are a modern development, but this one has been cultivated in China for thousands of years and is in the parentage of many modern miniatures. In colour it is softest pink. There are not many single miniatures, so I planted three each of 'Simplex' (single white), and 'Wee Beth' (an Australian-bred single, apricot pink). 'Dresden Doll' had to be included. It is a miniature Moss rose, and 'Popcorn', a diminutive semi-single white which reminds me of the flowers of feverfew. For contrast I added 'Baby Faurax' (deep purple) and 'Antique Rose', the dusty magenta-pink of old ladies' bonnets.

These little roses do need some attention to ensure the continuous blooming

LITTLE PORTION
WITH 'MRS
HERBERT STEVENS'
ON THE ARCH.

of which they are capable. I gave them a mulch of stable manure mixed with straw and a handful of blood and bone with ten per cent potash added in the spring. Even so they appreciated an occasional foliar feed and they do need adequate water. We installed a trickle watering system both to conserve water and to avoid wetting the leaves. Black spot looks unsightly on the little roses, and to avoid it some spraying seems to be inevitable. Pruning is no trouble, however. They can be severely treated each winter – with the shears, if you like.

As ground covers I used in the main a variety of low-growing thymes: *Thymus* 'Albus', *T.* 'Coccineus', *T.* 'Lars Hall' and, probably my favourite, the woolly thyme (*T. pseudolanuginosus*); also alyssum (*Lobularia maritima*). All seeded themselves generously and in no time made a fragrant carpet among the brick paving.

The tiny bulbs came up through the ground covers each year: *Cyclamen hederifolium* and *Cyclamen coum* for autumn colour, and in the spring, before the roses come into bloom, English primroses, auriculas, crocus and species tulips. Also a tiny, miniature aquilegia (*Aquilegia bertolinii*) and a variety of small iris: *Iris setosa nana*, *Iris gracilipes* and *Iris graminea*.

On the high lattice which surrounded this little formal area *Rosa banksiae* 'Lutea' and *R. banksiae* var. *banksiae* (the white, violet-perfumed, double form) formed a thick cover very quickly.

The Miniature Garden became a feature of Bleak House. Over the years the cottage itself has filled many purposes, as toolshed, as potting shed, for a while as a horticultural bookshop before a larger space was needed.

A winding path with mixed borders on either side links it to the main house and it was here that the botanical artist Jenny Phillips sat for many hours doing a delightful black and white drawing of the cottage, which we later used to print a bookplate.

It was in its second spring that a friend from Melbourne who had recently returned from a holiday in the Cotswolds saw the cottage and fell instantly in love with it.

'Does it have a name?' she asked. No, it did not.

'I have just had the holiday of my life in a little cottage just like it. Would you call it Little Portion?'

So Little Portion it remained.

CHAPTER
13

DAFFODILS

A Queenslander by birth, I shall never forget my first spring in Victoria. I had grown up in a garden of frangipani and hibiscus, the great scarlet umbrellas of the poincianas, banana palms, and mangoes to be picked from the edge of the verandah.
My mother had grown, with difficulty, in the coolest part of the garden, a few freesias, which she loved, but really we had no seasons. The garden was green and lush throughout the year so that I was totally unprepared for the glory that is spring in a cold climate, the reawakening, the burgeoning, the fresh young leaves and, above all, the carpets of bulbs. I resolved then and there that, if I ever had a garden of my own, I would grow bulbs, hundreds and thousands of bulbs.

The year before I bought Bleak House I had gone to Kyneton to visit a friend in hospital. Having arrived early, I had a few minutes to wait. In the garden I found a birdbath with a small bronze plaque with the inscription:

MRS E. MURRAY
THE JOY OF HER GARDEN
HAS BEEN OUR GAIN.

I asked the Sister-in-charge about Mrs Murray. She had a wonderful garden, I was told, and opened it each year at the time of the Kyneton Daffodil Festival in aid of the Hospital. The birdbath and plaque were a small gesture of thanks from the Hospital for years of support.

I missed the Festival the following year, taken up entirely with the initial work on Bleak House. But the following spring I determined to visit Eve Murray's garden.

I had to go through Kyneton and the whole little township was dressed for the Daffodil Festival; daffodils in beds all along the main streets; daffodils adorning every shop window; girls in long skirts, offering daffodils to all the visitors – in one case with a glass of sherry as well. I asked directions to Langley, which is a few kilometres out of the town, but I hardly needed to refer to them as there was a steady stream of cars going in the same direction. Murray's Road itself is lined thickly with daffodils. Not a thin ribbon of daffodils, but great sheets of gold under the gum trees which formed a canopy. They looked as much at home, I thought, as any of Wordsworth's daffodils.

The drive was packed with cars, and at the gate were collection boxes in aid of the Hospital. Little of the garden is visible from the gate, as one enters from the back, but as I came round the corner of the house I caught my breath.

The garden slopes away from the house down to a huge dam, and the slope was a sea of daffodils. Daffodils of every size, shape and colour, more varieties than I had ever dreamed might exist, and not a dozen or so of each variety but hundreds. The garden covers an area of one and a half to two hectares. At the base of the slope, Eve had planted, some forty-five years ago, an oak wood. All of the trees were grown from acorns, picked up wherever she could find them, and included a holm oak grown from an acorn found in the Adelaide Botanic Gardens. And the oak wood, too, was thickly planted with daffodils.

Afternoon tea was served on the verandah overlooking the garden, and here I met Eve Murray – in a wheelchair: tiny, white-haired, over eighty, with laughing eyes, a penetrating gaze and an absolutely indomitable spirit. Eve had come to Langley as a bride in 1931 to a house set in a paddock. She had immediately set about making a garden, at first watering her trees with buckets of water. A bore was put in in 1938, but the big dam not until 1960. I asked her when she had started gardening – 'from the moment I was born', she said. 'And I used to steal cuttings through the fences on the way home from school.'

A hedge of lilac and a low stone wall divide the garden horizontally. Above this, she told me, was intended to be 'a tidy garden' and below it, 'just fun'. But some-how it never quite worked out that way, and I think the whole garden became fun – a labour of love which has given intense pleasure to hundreds of people.

Eve's special interest in daffodils goes back a long way. Initially her aim had been to breed a pink daffodil and in this she succeeded. Unfortunately she seldom bothered to register the names of the daffodils she bred. Her own favourite among them is 'Philippa', white with a cream trumpet and named after her little grand-daughter. There was a splendid white one on display the day I visited the garden – 'Nell Robinson'.

There were hard times – drought, when there was no water to spare for the garden, for this is also a large sheep property. There was fire through the garden in 1944 which destroyed a lot of trees. And of latter years there has been illness.

Looking at the imposing trees enclosing the garden today, the enormous Judas tree (*Cercis siliquastrum*) grown from seed, the beautiful blue *Cedrus atlantica* 'Glauca' and the tall deodars, the almonds, the itea with its long greenish-yellow catkins, it is difficult to believe that fire wrought such destruction.

I stood on the verandah, looking down on the sea of gold stretching down to the dam, which was Eve's life's work. Among the daffodils were literally thousands of deep blue muscari and two magnificent white magnolias (*Magnolia stellata* and another I could not name). And over to the right, in startling contrast to the tra-ditional yellows, whites and blues of spring, was a bed of brilliant scarlet tulips. I have never liked scarlet as a colour, and usually avoid planting scarlet flowers in the garden, but on this afternoon I went home, thumbed through all my bulb cata-logues and ordered thirty *Tulipa fosteriana* 'Red Emperor' for the next year.

Bulbs, I was convinced, were the perfect companions for my roses. They would provide colour in the spring, long before the roses sent forth their first buds, and, if I chose carefully, I could have autumn-flowering bulbs also, when the old roses were finished.

A good many bulbs like the same open, sunny position as roses do, and if I carried out my scheme of watering with a trickle system, I could have an emitter for each rose and let the bulbs have the dry conditions they need in summer.

I had bought some bulbs from Eve Murray's garden (in aid of the Kyneton Hospital) – some twenty or thirty – but this would go nowhere in the space I wanted to fill. I needed to acquire them by the hundred – or by the thousand.

All through this part of Victoria – the Gold Centre – are the remains of little cottages – some rough stone, some weatherboard – built in the booming gold rush days when these little villages were busy, bustling townships, and long since abandoned. Often a little cluster of old fruit trees is the only sign that here was once a cottage. And under the fruit trees are nearly always bulbs – jonquils and daffodils and snowflakes. Often, after a hundred years of neglect, of never being lifted, the daffodils have become double and sometimes tinged with green. These I loved.

There was one particular little weatherboard cottage I passed often. Deserted long since, its windows were broken and the door hung disconsolately on one hinge. But, improbably, the brilliant lipstick-pink climbing rose 'Nancy Hayward' still flowered bravely on the derelict verandah posts and over the verandah roof right up to the chimney. And the ground was carpeted each spring by daffodils. Here was the sort of supply I needed.

So I set out to find the owner of the cottage, if, indeed, there was one. Enquiries at the local general store elicited a flood of information. It belonged to old Mrs Miller. Her husband had died some years back and anyhow they hadn't lived in that cottage for twenty years. Lived in the village, she did, with a pack of savage dogs. The storekeeper shook his head. Eccentric, she was. Some said – and he made an expressive gesture of his hand towards his forehead. Well, he concluded, no one went there if they didn't have to. Against his will, he gave me directions to her cottage and, clearly puzzled, added further emphatic warnings about the dogs.

I went to visit her the following Saturday. Her cottage stood alone at the end of the village. With difficulty I unbound the wire from the front gate and went up the steps to the front door. As I did so, the dogs emerged from round the back – a mangy, underfed, snarling pack. I was profoundly thankful for the fence which divided off the front garden.

I knocked loudly, realising as I did so that probably no one ever came to the front door. There was no response. I tried again. And again. Just as I was about to give up – wild horses would not have got me to the back door, for that would have meant braving the dogs – round the corner of the house came the dirtiest human being I had ever encountered. She was dressed in rags, a man's old felt hat pulled low over her forehead and men's old boots on her feet, hostility written all over her.

Abruptly she asked my business. 'You own the old cottage at the other end of the village?' I asked.

'And what if I do?' came the reply.

I explained that I was making a garden and I wanted to plant daffodils. Could I buy some of her bulbs?

She half turned away, and there was such a long pause I thought I was going to get no answer at all. Finally it came in what amounted to a snarl: 'I don't want your money.'

I tried again. I explained that they were expensive to buy from nurseries and I needed a lot. I loved the old simple ones, especially the double ones, better than the sophisticated, developed varieties. I was prepared to offer her a fair price. Even as I said it, I was aware that money was not her chief concern. Perhaps she still loved the old cottage. Perhaps its garden had been important to her.

Again a pause. Finally – 'You can 'ave the bulbs. But I don't want your money.'

I asked if there was, then, something I could do for her.

'You can bring me a bucket of bulbs' she said as she turned away.

I took a collection of cartons with me and, for four hours, I dug bulbs – mostly daffodils, a few jonquils. There were old roses along the front fence and I took some cuttings. 'Félicité et Perpétue' was growing over an old shed. It turns up in many of the old gardens in this part of Victoria. I suppose, since it strikes so easily from cuttings, that it was given from hand to hand in the early days.

My cartons full, and loaded into the car, I dug a 'bucket o' bulbs' for old Mrs Miller. Then I went back to the general store. The storekeeper was incredulous.

'You never went up there?' he asked.

I assured him that I had indeed and asked if Mrs Miller ever came to the shop. 'Now and again' was the response. I asked what sort of things she bought.

'Chocolate biscuits' came the prompt reply. 'Always chocolate biscuits.'

So I bought a whole carton of chocolate biscuits. Not being anxious to encounter either Mrs Miller or her dogs again, I deposited the carton and the 'bucket o' bulbs' at the front door and fled.

The following year – with more beds to fill – I went back. She remembered me and was almost cordial.

'You take as many as you like,' she said. And, yes, she wouldn't mind a few more herself.

This time, when I took them to her (together with another carton of chocolate biscuits) I planted them for her – thickly, along the edge of the front verandah. I did not see her again, nor did I try to, but each year, as I pass her cottage in spring, I am glad to see the daffodils still in bloom.

And as I look at them in my own garden, flowering more abundantly each year, I wonder afresh about old Mrs Miller. Perhaps, like Eve Murray, she had gone as a bride to that little cottage and the daffodils and the roses along the fence had been planted when she was young and her heart full of dreams.

CHAPTER

14

WATER

W ater, it was apparent from the outset, would be a matter of prime concern. And it was a problem which would have to be tackled sooner rather than later.

Malmsbury has an annual rainfall of approximately 70 centimetres, and most of it falls in the winter. The summers are long, and dry, and hot, and farming activities in the area are all geared to 'the autumn break' which comes, as a rule, towards the end of March. So the summer months are critical for a garden.

Bleak House is too far out to be served by the town supply and when I bought the property the only water came from the old windmill beside the house. This was sweet water and perfectly adequate for domestic use, but it would never do for a large garden.

Water transforms a landscape. When the lake came up in the winter, the view over the paddocks was splendid. But in the summer, when the lake had dried up and the grass turned brown, the eye sought the relief of water. And there was none. So I thought in terms of dams and contacted a local bulldozer driver to discuss putting in a dam, not too far from the garden, to serve both practical and aesthetic purposes.

I had one very good neighbour, Norman Ward, who owned an imposing four-storied bluestone mill between Bleak House and Kyneton. Norm's family had owned the mill since 1860, and Norm, having lived and farmed here all his life, was regarded as an authority on most rural matters. He came to visit me the day the bulldozer driver came. When he heard of the projected dam, he shook his head and said with the innate conservatism of farmers the world over, 'It's not dam country. It's bore country. Nobody round here goes in for dams.'

Now bores may be very efficient but they do nothing for the landscape. I had a mental vision of a sheet of water (with waterlilies, of course) surrounded by trees and water iris, a veritable oasis in the midst of the plains.

Finally we compromised. Noel Jennings (a treasure beyond price, and the only artistic bulldozer driver of my acquaintance) would build a small dam, a $500 dam, and I would get in touch with a contractor who would put down a bore.

As it must be done in the summer while the ground is dry, work began on the dam immediately. Simultaneously, the contractor arrived to put down the bore. Bores cost so much per metre, so, as there is no way of knowing in advance how deep they will have to go before they strike water, there is no way of estimating the cost. I spent an anxious morning, rushing from dam to bore and watching the progress of both.

The bulldozer struck rock and shale at a depth of about three metres, so could go no deeper. The clay was put back, the topsoil neatly piled up for future use, the biggest rocks – and they were very big – strategically placed round the banks. I had my first dam.

The bore struck water at about thirty metres, quite a good flow, and later analysis proved it to be sweet and suitable for stock or garden.

An electrically-driven pressure pump was installed at the bore head and a petrol-driven one (to give two strings to the bow in case of electrical failure) on the banks of the (still dry) dam. A plumber was called in to take the water from the electric pump to taps all round the garden and I felt that I was ready to face the next summer.

Water was, without doubt, the biggest expenditure involved in setting up the garden. And I was by no means finished. Trickle lines would have to be installed in all garden beds as they were constructed. Sprinklers are really not feasible under my conditions. They use far too much water, a good deal of which goes where it is not needed, and it evaporates quickly if used during the day. Furthermore, over-head watering does encourage black spot in roses.

The following weekend, with my mind still running very much on water, I went for an evening walk in the biggest of the quarries. I loved the solitude, the great moss-covered boulders, the view towards Mount Macedon and to the back of the house. And there, in the midst of the quarry, I came upon a hitherto undiscovered waterhole. This was January, and a stone thrown into the water indicated that it was still very deep. Round the margin were elderberry bushes (*Sambucus nigra*) with their flat ivory-coloured flower heads and clusters of berries, some of which were just now starting to turn black. And there was *Rosa canina*, the little dog rose, which must have escaped from gardens in the early days and has become something of a pest to farmers. I regarded it as anything but a pest. Here, ready-made, was the vision I had had in my mind's eye when I decided to put in a dam. It was, of course, too far from the house to be of any practical use, nor could it be seen until one stumbled upon it, but it was, in itself, beautiful. And perhaps it indicated the presence of a spring.

My two blue heelers, good mates, affectionate and excitable, great chasers of rabbits, accompanied me on all walks. The little bitch loved water so, with her usual precipitateness, she plunged in. Now this waterhole was formed by quarrying, so the banks all round were of steep stone. Cara, her desire for a swim gratified, found she could not scramble up the sheer stone banks. Willy, a goodtime boy if ever there was one, lay on a flat stone at the top and watched, offering no assistance. By lying flat on a rock, I finally managed to seize her front paws and haul her out, though there was an anxious moment when I felt she was about to haul me in.

I thought about that waterhole all the way home. This was exactly what I wanted in my 'extended landscape', but close to the house. If water could be held all summer in the quarry, then why not on the flat ground which became a lake each winter.

Remembering the role of the State Rivers and Water Authority in the matter of the tip, I contacted them and asked for advice. They could not have been more helpful – even when they found my purpose in all this was far from utilitarian. They assumed initially that I wanted to drain the land and use it for farming purposes. This, they explained, would be very expensive. Quite the reverse was what I had in mind. I wanted to keep the water, so that the waterbirds, instead of flying away each summer when the lake dried up, might be persuaded to make their homes there, in a safe haven.

They tested the soil, examined the ground thoroughly and advised me finally that if I built a chain of waterholes across the lake the water could probably be retained and, an added bonus, the winter flooding would be reduced.

So Noel Jennings was consulted again. Had he been born half a century later, I feel sure he would have done a course and qualified as a landscape architect. He was a practising one in any case.

He constructed an enormous waterhole in the middle of the now dry lake. It had bays and inlets and a large island for the birds to nest on. And in the middle of the job Noel came up to the house one day to report that, in the midst of a dry hot February, he had become bogged. He had, indeed, struck a spring and water seeped in, slowly and steadily throughout March – to my infinite satisfaction.

In the autumn we planted the edges – this was a lake, not a dam, so no need to worry about the effects of roots on a dam wall – with several varieties of willow: the weeping willow (*Salix babylonica*), the tortured willow (*Salix matsudana* 'Tortuosa'), the pussy willow (*Salix caprea*) and the basket willow (*Salix viminalis*), which grows all along the banks of the Campaspe River.

But I wanted trees on the island also, and getting there posed a problem. So I bought, the following spring, a small rowing boat. With difficulty, for I have no natural talents in this direction, I learnt to row it. Long spring evenings were spent planting up the island.

Full of optimism I planted a swamp cypress (*Taxodium distichum*) but, sadly, it did not survive the first summer. A seedling apple did much better and several roots of *Rosa indica major*, often regarded as a form of *R. chinensis*. Much used as a rootstock in the early days, it has survived in many of our country cemeteries, defying all efforts of Shire workers 'cleaning up' to eradicate it. *Rosa multiflora*, also, seemed impervious to drought, flood, frost, sun and wind. Graham Stuart Thomas, in his delightful book *A Garden of Roses* wrote of it that 'on account of its dense, arching, but bushy growth and ease of cultivation, it is used to prevent soil erosion and as a crash-barrier on motorways.' He added that 'its heps provide nourishment for birds'. What more could one ask? It flourished on the island and I hope that, by now, the birds are indeed feeding on the heps.

In my early experiments with herbs as ground covers among the roses, I had planted, seduced by its fern-like foliage and flat white flower heads, some roots of the common achillea (*Achillea millefolium*). To my eternal sorrow, it proved to be all but ineradicable. In my efforts to discourage it, I weeded it out by the armful and transported much of it to the island. Here it could (and did) ramp away to its heart's content.

The walk to the lake at sunset on summer Sunday evenings became something of a ritual over the next couple of years. I would set out (accompanied by the heelers, of course) row across to the island, and water, with buckets, all that was planted there. The dogs loved it, swimming across and then landing, wet and dirty, in the boat asking to be rowed back.

Later we put in another dam near the smallest of the quarries, which is not far from the house, and another bore with a windmill – always with the hope that here, some day, there would be a garden in a quarry. I planted a blue cedar (*Cedrus atlantica* 'Glauca') and two deodars (*Cedrus deodara*). Hugh Johnson, in his invaluable *Encyclopedia of Trees*, states that they usually take twenty years to reach a height of thirteen metres, but I reminded myself of the wonderful story of Thomas Jefferson who decided, at the age of eighty, to plant an avenue of oaks. The head gardener, when consulted, suggested tentatively, with Jefferson's age in mind, that oaks took a very long time to reach maturity. 'Right,' said Jefferson, 'then you'd better start this afternoon.'

Neither of these big waterholes was close enough to be of any use for the garden. They were intended for the birds (and incidentally for the sheep we agisted to keep the grass down and prevent it from becoming a fire hazard in the summer) and for their contribution to the landscape.

Much later, as the garden was extended, I put in a very big dam for watering purposes and installed another petrol-driven pump. It had a small island in it with a crab-apple tree (*Malus spectabilis* this time) and daffodils, and we planted self - sown seedlings of the white Rugosa rose, gathered up from all round the garden, round its margin. In the spring after this dam was constructed, the first black swans stayed and brought up their cygnets.

CHAPTER
15

MOSSES AND
NOISETTES

did, after all, order some Moss roses in that first year. For many people they and the Centifolias are the ones that first come to mind when one mentions 'old roses'. Small wonder that they so closely resemble each other for the Common Moss, introduced into England from the Continent early in the eighteenth century, is thought to have been a sport of *R. centifolia*.

With admirable restraint, and influenced, perhaps, by the disparaging remarks I had read about their being sprawling, lanky plants of dubious garden value, I limited myself, in this first order, to seven. And a truly masculine collection they were.

Into the very feminine company of Duchesses, Queens, Countesses and Madames who inhabited my garden I proposed now to introduce 'Général Kléber', 'James Mitchell', 'Henri Martin', 'Alfred de Dalmas', 'William Lobb', 'Chapeau de Napoléon' – and the exquisite 'Madame Louis Lévêque'.

Released, most of them, in the 1850s and 1860s, they were beloved by the Victorians, by gardeners, painters, embroidresses, and the makers of picture post-cards and valentines.

Historical associations and the exotic winged buds which resemble a cockaded hat made 'Chapeau de Napoléon' a 'must'. It is often classed not as a Moss but as a Centifolia; indeed its proper name is *R. centifolia* 'Cristata'. The brownish-green moss enhances the beauty of the silvery pink buds and the flowers fade to a lilac-pink as they age. Strange, that such an enchanting rose should be a chance seedling. It was discovered, so Graham Stuart Thomas tells us, in the crevice of an old wall at Fribourg in Switzerland.

Beside it I planted 'Général Kléber', named for the General whom Napoleon left behind to look after his army in Egypt. If ever a rose deserved the name of a beautiful woman it is this one. The fragrant flowers are the clearest, softest pink. Gordon Edwards describes it as 'mother-of-pearl pink'. They are produced on a bushy plant with fresh, green foliage and the buds are endowed with ample moss. I only wish it flowered for longer.

'James Mitchell' makes an attractive bush with long, arching canes and a profusion of small, tight pink flowers, each with a button eye. 'Henri Martin' is a clear and striking crimson – a great splash of colour. And 'William Lobb' is one of the very richest, a deep crimson-purple which fades to soft lavender. The bush is lanky and uncontrolled and, as it will grow to two and a half metres, it really needs some support, either from other plants or from a tripod. I have seen it looking positively splendid at Kiftsgate, intertwined with the rambler 'Albertine', against a mellow old brick wall.

'Alfred de Dalmas' (also known as 'Mousseline') and 'Madame Louis Lévêque' have the great virtue of being recurrent flowering. Both soft pink, and both sweetly scented, they are worthy of a place in any garden.

Having gone so far as to include the Mosses, I decided to order, in addition, some of the Noisette roses. I did want some recurrent flowering roses included in this first planting.

There is (as always) some disagreement about the origins of the Noisettes, but the most generally accepted version is that the original one was 'Champney's Pink Cluster', the rose I planted over the front door of Little Portion. This originated in 1802 on the property of a wealthy rice grower from South Carolina, John Champney, who was also a keen gardener. His rose was the result (most probably) of a cross, whether intentional or not, between *R. moschata* and the China rose, 'Old Blush', also known as 'Parson's Pink'. It bears great clusters of semi-double, highly perfumed little soft pink roses, and will climb to a height of four to five metres.

John Champney's neighbour in Carolina was one Philippe Noisette, a member of a family of Parisian rosarians, and he sent seedlings of the original rose to France. From these seedlings stems the family of Noisette roses, still highly prized by gardeners today.

Two of them I would include in that small (but sometimes varying) group of roses which I could not possibly be without. 'Lamarque' I had fallen in love with some years earlier. In the garden of Helen Vellacott in Castlemaine it grows right to the top of a giant *Magnolia grandiflora* and fills the whole garden with its distinctive, slightly lemony fragrance. It produces its creamy-white flowers over a period of many months, and the fresh green foliage is in itself beautiful.

'Madame Alfred Carrière' I met for the first time in that same garden. It is an old garden, a rambling country garden where things grow over and into one another, and the ground is a carpet of bulbs in the spring. Birds nest here and an old weeping elm whose branches come right down to the ground makes a secret place beloved by children. 'Madame Alfred Carrière' was already a very Senior Citizen when I first met her here, but the great bush, three metres wide and four metres high, was simply covered in softest blush-pink blooms which fade to white in the sunshine and scent the whole garden. She grew here in semi-shade under tall trees where the books say roses do not flourish. 'Madame Alfred' defied them all.

I had taken cuttings from this old bush the year before and they had grown. I resolved to plant the tiny bushes along the south side of the high carport I had had built beside the house – a carport with an attic and a gabled roof which was in keeping with the old house. The little roses got only an hour or so of early morning sun and the full blast of the south wind, but they reached the top of the attic over the carport within three years and were a never-ending source of delight. Each year at pruning time I find myself putting in cuttings for no better reason than that it seems such a wicked waste to throw away so much potential beauty.

And, as with my many cuttings of 'Albertine', there always seems to be another corner just suited to 'Madame Alfred', or another friend who has not yet realised what a treasure she is.

'Desprez à fleur jaune', soft buff yellow with apricot-pink overtones, and 'Alister Stella Gray', creamy-yellow paling to white, battled manfully with the cold wet winters and became great favourites.

'Maréchal Niel' I had no luck with, although I tried twice. I think he really did find the Malmsbury winters too much for him. They say in England he must be grown under glass. He struggled valiantly each time for a year or two and produced a few lovely soft yellow, scented blooms. I had put him to grow over a shade house so that one could look up at him from underneath. Had he flourished the effect would have been all that I desired, but each winter he grew pale and wan and finally gave up the ghost.

'Aimée Vibert' I could not enthuse over. The little pink buds are charming, as are the clusters of small white roses, but she does die in the most unattractive fashion and it is essential to cut off the bunches of brown heads which spoil the whole effect – a difficult task to keep up in a large garden. Perhaps my dislike of her was influenced by other factors. She played a key role in one of my most conspicuous garden failures.

In an old garden magazine I had come upon a picture of a maypole made of roses. It was enchanting. This was a splendid way to grow climbers. So I set about designing one. I chose a sheltered spot – as sheltered as I could provide. It had an

'DAYDREAM'– NOT PLIABLE ENOUGH FOR A MAYPOLE – WITH LITTLE PORTION IN THE BACKGROUND.

old cypress on the south side at the foot of which I had planted 'Bloomfield Courage' and 'Wedding Day'. The dark green of the cypress provided the ideal foil for the dark red and white of the clusters of single roses. A Rugosa hedge gave some shelter from the west and on the east there was the shadehouse which bounded the projected Yellow Garden.

We set a large bush pole firmly in the ground as a centrepost and from it took eight wires to the circumference of a circle. These were attached to steel posts driven right into the ground. The area underneath was paved with bluestone set on black plastic and sand as I was sure that once the roses grew it would be quite impossible to weed underneath.

There was nothing wrong with the construction, but the whole thing never worked as I had intended. In the first place I think I chose the wrong roses. 'Aimée Vibert' simply refused to grow up the wires. She preferred to make a large shrub. 'Daydream's' canes were not sufficiently pliable and 'Shot Silk', which came to me from the grower as a climber, turned out to be bush after all. The only one that did as she was meant to do was *Rosa × leonida*, formerly known as 'Marie Léonida'. Released in 1842 and thought to be a hybrid between *R. bracteata* and *R. laevigata*, she has long pliable canes, glossy dark green foliage and very double rounded creamy-white roses.

In addition to the fact that I think I chose the wrong roses – ramblers would have been far more appropriate – I think, being in the middle of a 'lawn' and hence not part of a trickle system, they never got enough of either food or water. I am sure that the idea was feasible and I would love to try it again with the benefit of experience.

So 'Aimée Vibert' was not popular on this account. Added to this, it was she who harboured my first snake in the garden.

I was going to Melbourne and went down to turn off the tap near 'Aimée Vibert' and there, in front of her, basking in the late afternoon sun, was a large copperhead. I stopped dead. The first essential was to put the dogs away. Cara, who chased anything that moved, was sure to be as silly about snakes as she was about waterholes and magpies. I called them in my most peremptory fashion and succeeded in shutting them both in the kitchen.

I had been presented with a shotgun – a Winchester .410 – it being, I was informed, an essential piece of equipment for one who made a practice of walking in snake-infested quarries. Now I have no natural affinity with guns and always have to stop and think which eye it is I have to close to look along the barrel! I took it down now and loaded it deliberately and with exaggerated care, hoping all the while that by the time I returned the snake would have gone.

But there he lay, watching me, I felt sure, with an intuitive knowledge of my intentions. I had owned the gun for two years or more and never used it except for some target practice in the paddock, shooting at a kerosene tin which I invariably missed. I hated the thought of killing anything. I tried to see the copperhead through D. H. Lawrence's eyes. I tried to envisage the beauty of the one that came to his water-trough to drink and he 'in pyjamas for the heat'. But I thought instead of Cara and Willy and the final line of Kenneth Mackenzie's poem 'and in its mouth it carries death'. Strengthened in my resolve, I put the gun to my shoulder, closed I'm not sure which eye – possibly both – and pulled the trigger. As the little puff of smoke and cloud of dust cleared away I saw, to my utter astonishment, that this time I had hit my target.

CHAPTER 14

THE YELLOW GARDEN

t was *R. foetida* 'Bicolor' which was responsible for the birth of the Yellow Garden. When I first saw a bush of it, with its bright green foliage and mass of little single roses with petals bright coppery-scarlet on top and soft, butterscotch-yellow underneath, it was a case of love at first sight. I simply had to have it.

Why it is familiarly known as 'Austrian Copper' is a mystery to me. It is a sport of the almost equally enchanting *R. foetida*, known as the 'Austrian Briar', whose flowers are like little enamelled buttercups. Both appear to have had their origins somewhere in western Asia – certainly not in Austria. Perhaps they were brought in stages from one part of the Ottoman Empire to another in the way that many plants have travelled along the Old Silk Road from China to Persia. Neither can I hazard a guess as to why they are called '*foetida*' for their scent, while by no means your usual rose scent, I find in no way unpleasant.

The decision had been taken. I had to find a place for both of them somewhere in the garden, but those brilliant yellows from the East have no affinity with the soft pinks, the rosy-purples and deep wine colours of the old, European roses.

There was nothing for it. I would have to extend the garden and make a special place for them.

I had been thinking for some time that I needed a shadehouse. Every owner of a fairly large garden comes to this conclusion sooner or later. Plants are needed in quantity – not in ones or twos. And buying twenty of this and thirty of that from nurseries is out of the question. Propagating becomes an essential part of running the garden. I wanted something quite simple – just somewhere out of the hot sun to put cuttings and plants which were too small to be planted out yet. Plastic tunnels – while no doubt very functional – are anathema to me. I wanted something which would merge into the garden.

So I decided to place the Yellow Garden to the north of the Miniature Garden. A lattice fence was already in place there and would form the southern boundary and – with Albert's invaluable assistance – I erected my shadehouse to cut the Yellow Garden off on the western side. We made it of bush poles and treated pine lattice, like three pergolas in the shape of a rectangle with the centre and the long eastern side open. It was thus protected from north, south and west winds (we got all three!) but open to the morning sun. We roofed it with lattice and, rather than using shadecloth, I planted that dear little white rambler 'Félicité et Perpétue' round three sides of it. Rev. S. Reynolds Hole (Dean of Rochester) refers to it as 'Félicité Perpétuelle' (a most appropriate name) and speaks of it 'climbing heaven-wards in emblematic beauty'. It quickly formed a dense cover, looked breath-taking each spring and, being almost evergreen, afforded protection not only from the hot sun but also from winter frosts. I gave the whole structure a touch of formality by planting four pencil pines in the inner corners and, in the open centre, a one and a half metre weeping standard 'Orange Cascade', the little miniature rose I had used in the front garden, which is not orange at all but a deep golden yellow.

In my yellow garden I planted two each of *R. foetida* and *R. foetida* 'Bicolor' and one of the double form, *R. foetida* 'Persiana'. Quite in keeping with them is the dramatic red 'Geranium', a seedling of the species rose *R. moyesii,* and raised by the Royal Horticultural Society at Wisley. That great rosarian Roy Shepherd des-cribed *R. moyesii* as being 'one of the most desirable of all rose species in blossom, colour, foliage and fruits'. 'Geranium' is very like its parent. Its single deep scarlet flowers made it the ideal companion for *R. foetida* 'Bicolor' and, after a brilliant flowering, it produces equally brilliant flagon-shaped, scarlet hips which hang on right into winter.

Here, too, I found a home for 'Mutabilis', sometimes thought to be a species

A TOUCH OF FORMALITY - 'CRÉPUSCULE' ON THE LEFT, A WEEPING STANDARD OF 'ORANGE CASCADE' AND 'PAUL TRANSON' ON THE RIGHT.

ABOVE: A SPLASH OF SCARLET FROM 'GERANIUM'.

LEFT: 'CHARLES AUSTIN' IN FRONT OF THE BIG PINE NEAR THE GATE INTO THE YELLOW GARDEN.

rose but probably an old chance hybrid from a Chinese garden. It is unlike any other rose. The buds are vivid orange, then open to a single, soft yellow rose which, as it ages, goes through pink to quite deep red. It flowers continuously, so that at almost any time all colours are on the bush simultaneously. I found it did not much like our harsh frosts and did better later when the garden had grown up a little and it had some shelter from a young apple tree. At the foot of that same apple I planted one of the loveliest of all red roses (I had almost written *the* loveliest of all red roses, but then I thought of 'Charles de Mills') 'Château de Clos Vougeot', which I had grown to love in Maria's garden.

I had an ambition to grow *R. × hemisphaerica*, the Sulphur Rose, but it proved to be a piece of arrant folly. The combination of our harsh conditions and my inexperience discouraged it utterly and, after producing one or two miserable flowers it gave up the ghost entirely.

I covered the eastern fence, against the paddocks, with the evergreen *R. laevigata* (the Cherokee Rose). It took a couple of winters before it adapted to the cold, but then proceeded to produce masses of its pure single white blooms with their golden stamens early in each spring, and its glossy, dark green leaves formed a dense, if thorny, cover for the fence. In front of it I planted hundreds (literally) of the soft mauve-blue iris which we used to call '*Iris stylosa*' but is now *Iris unguicularis*. They made a patch of colour when most things are dormant in mid-winter.

White agapanthus lined the main path and I found their green seed-heads were a wonderful foil for the scarlet hips of 'Geranium' and for the less showy, but nonetheless very effective, hips of *R. × alba* 'Semi-plena'. For the same reasons I planted two of the little white Rugosa rose, 'Schneezwerg' (Snow Dwarf).

The area needed trees. I decided on four quinces (*Cydonia oblonga*). Their blush-pink, single blooms must be one of the loveliest of all spring blossoms and fortunately they come well before my scarlet and yellow roses. As an added bonus, their glowing golden fruits hang like great globes in the trees in late summer.

Apricot-coloured roses were at home here, too: 'Alchymist', with its great flat quartered blooms; 'Crépuscule', the delightful little rich apricot Noisette rose, constantly in flower but appreciating some frost protection; 'Paul Transon', a copper-coloured hybrid of that very versatile *R. wichuraiana*, which my English books said 'might sometimes repeat in autumn', but which unfailingly does so for us; and that strange, milk-coffee-coloured modern, 'Julia's Rose', which I found much more rewarding as a climber than as a bush. I put four of the great, scarlet, single climbing rose 'Altissimo' to grow through 'Félicité et Perpétue' on the shadehouse.

The Yellow Garden, having been started more or less as an afterthought, became a much-loved part of the garden. Scarlet 'Red Emperor' tulips were planted here; cherry-coloured ixias, found along the roadside at Taradale; the scarlet *Haemanthus coccineus*, whose huge, strap-like leaves have earned it the name of 'elephant's ears', flowered for a year or so but then mysteriously disappeared; the snake's head iris (*Hermodactylus tuberosus*) with its strange olive-green and black flowers; the barber's pole oxalis with its starry white flowers and cheerful red and white striped buds (definitely not invasive).

White daffodils were planted here and the white form of muscari; the white lychnis (*Lychnis coronaria* 'Alba') with its silvery-grey foliage; *Spiloxene capensis*, whose strange, star-like flowers with a brown and green stripe on the undersurface of the petals unfold in bright sunshine while you watch them.

In parts of the Yellow Garden were great slabs of moss-covered rock with only pockets of soil between. I wound the path in and out around them, filled the pockets with compost and planted yellow and orange and rust-coloured day-lilies (*Hemerocallis*). All were gifts from friends' gardens and I never knew their names, but they flourished and multiplied and made a brave show every summer, with a very minimum of care.

And then there were the great spotted orange tiger lilies (*Lilium lancifolium* syn. *L. tigrinum*), which shrieked at everything else in the garden. I had never liked them but had been given a quantity the previous year and had spent at least an hour wandering round the garden with the bulbs in a bucket, wondering what on earth I could do with them. Finally, in desperation, and consoling myself with the thought that they might not be noticed there, I planted them at the very back of the rockery. They flowered, of course, triumphantly, right beside the soft pink climber 'Blossomtime'. It was not to be tolerated. They would have to go.

'BLOSSOMTIME' –
ALWAYS IN FLOWER.

And then I went to Smeaton. I was looking, as usual, for roses planted in old gardens. I had seen pictures of the old, five-storied bluestone mill and heard stories of its garden. It had been built in 1860 on the banks of Birch Creek by a man named Anderson, who had had the fore-thought to plant the banks of the stream with oaks – they are towering giants today, and provide a perfect setting for the old stone building. And Andersons had lived and gardened there ever since.

I climbed the hill and pushed open the picket gate between two towering poplars. In true cottage garden fashion the path led straight to the front door. But this was no contrived, re-production cottage garden. This was the genuine article, the result of one hundred years of gardening by one family. The path was narrow and plants spilled over in generous profusion, reducing it sometimes to little over half a metre in width. Love-in-the-mist was here, and daisies violas and hollyhocks, sweet peas on a high trellis, flowering as they seemed to do when I was a child, and lavateras, their delicate petals acquiring an almost luminous quality in the shade of a giant liquidambar. This seemed to disprove all the theories about liquidambars being unsuitable in gardens as they rob the soil to too great an extent, for cottage plants clustered all about its feet. Currants, red and black, were there in plenty, and gooseberries, conjuring up smells of country cooking and visions of pantry shelves laden with bottles of preserved fruit and jams. And there was a twisted old

Granny Smith, its branches weighed down with the weight of its fruit. I'm sure it is seldom pruned.

Lynette Anderson was interested in my quest. Yes, they had old roses, some of them dating back to the building of the house. This was in the gold rush days. It had been intended that the house, like the mill, should be built of local stone, but in all the excitement consequent upon the discovery of gold, this was put off and a weatherboard house built instead. Looking at the pretty roof-line, the wide verandah across the front, the curving bargeboards and big chimneys, I could not feel that much had been lost.

The roses were growing, in the way old roses look best, among cottage plants. Some were flowering at the time of my visit, although the very old ones were over. It is unimportant, in a garden such as this, if they flower only in the spring. Surrounded by lavenders, nepetas, dianthus and herbs, they fade into the background once their flowering period is over, until their hips appear. They were known to Lynette seldom by their registered names, but rather by the names of their donors, so that the garden was full of daily reminders of friends and relatives. I was given cuttings of a little pink rose, known simply as 'Auntie Clark's Rose', and a deep, purplish-crimson Moss rose, not in flower at the time but described at teatime as having 'the colour of Noel Coward's jacket on this record-cover'. It turned out to be 'William Lobb', known in our gardens since 1855 but quite the latest thing, I suppose, when this gnarled old bush was planted.

We had tea in the high-ceilinged dining room on a cedar table with a white linen cloth. It was hand-embroidered with flowers and seemed to bring the garden right into the house. Then, through the window, I saw the tiger lilies, a whole army of them. Tall and arrogant, they tossed their tawny heads above a sea of golden and orange marigolds and yellow daisies – and here, in the right company, they looked splendid.

So my tiger lilies, too, found a home in the Yellow Garden. But in place of the marigolds (I like neither the feel nor the scent of them), I planted cream, yellow and orange eschscholzias. They seed themselves and come back year after year. If I had made its acquaintance at that time, I would also have planted the soft yellow *Anthemis* 'E. C. Buxton'. But I did not meet her until some years later.

LOUIE WILSON'S LEGACY

*T*he Yellow Garden had benefited from my visit to Smeaton but it was, in fact, quite another quest which had first taken me to this sleepy, forgotten little goldfields town.

In a book entitled *Historic Gardens of Victoria,* by Peter Watts, which came out in 1983, I had come upon a short account of Camnethan Homestead near Smeaton. It was described as a garden 'full of reminders of past glory' and 'one of the most elaborate small gardens known to have existed in Victoria'.

The accompanying photograph showed a straight central path edged in box leading to a cottage with a roof-line very like that of Bleak House and, to the left of the path, the most enchanting summerhouse – circular with Gothic arches.

Garden structures fascinate me and I am congenitally unable to resist anything which bears any resemblance to a Gothic arch. I was, in addition, still very much exercised as to how much formality can successfully be introduced into an Australian country garden without its becoming incongruous. I determined to seek out Camnethan Homestead.

Smeaton is in Central Victoria, not very far from Ballarat and about an hour's drive from Malmsbury. The town is tiny. A little bridge leads over the river near the Andersons' mill. There are a few fine old buildings, the Post Office and a General Store and not much else. I enquired at both the Post Office and the store, but no-one had heard of Camnethan and I did not know the name of the present occupant. Any mention of a fine old garden met with looks of puzzlement and dubious shakings of the head. I drove unsuccessfully round the outskirts of the town and finally, with no feeling of optimism, approached a large woman out hosing her garden, a brilliant affair of orange and scarlet Hybrid Teas, marigolds and zinnias. Concrete edges enclosed geometrically shaped beds, colourful pots lined the concrete drive and a pair of large concrete emus presided over the whole.

I mentioned Camnethan. To my surprise she nodded her head. 'Yes,' she said, 'old Louie Wilson' s place. Lives out there by herself. Never comes into the town now. She's well over ninety.' Camnethan, she informed me, lay some miles outside the town but, she assured me, with a rather pitying smile and a glance full of pride at her own creation, there was no garden there.

I drove, according to her directions, along an unpromising dirt track and came ultimately to a wire gate hanging loose on its hinges with the name 'Camnethan' just decipherable on a wooden board. It looked as though my informant might have been right. It was difficult to believe that here had once been a notable garden. An overgrown tree-lined drive led round to the back of the house. No sign of a vehicle in the tumbledown shed. Not even a dog or the dusty white hens usually found pecking round the back yard of an Australian farmhouse.

However, a knock on the back door was answered by a tiny, white-haired, smiling old woman who introduced herself simply as 'Louie' and, despite the fact that I was a complete stranger, welcomed me in. Louie was deaf, so it was with difficulty that I got her to understand that I had read about her garden and was interested in old roses.

She shook her head sadly and explained that there was no garden left. She was ninety-five years old and the garden had been made by her late husband's grand-father. On a hasty calculation I estimated that that put it back well into the last century. Louie was a newcomer to the property, she explained. She had lived here only for the last twenty-five years! For a long time now there had been no one here except herself, no one to tend the garden.

However, she had some photographs of the garden as it had been. She looked in vain through all the drawers in her desk but finally had to abandon the search. I prevailed upon her to let me see, instead, what remained of the garden.

We had to go through the main part of the house, which was clearly no longer in use – faded, water-stained wallpapers, lace curtains yellow with age, antimacas-sars, tasselled velvet cushions, marks of damp on the ceilings and family portraits on the wall. It was hard to open the front door with its huge old iron key and rusty bolts. But when it finally swung open there, bathed in afternoon sunlight, was the garden – a desolate jungle of long grass and tangled vines, the remains of a large wooden arch lying across the path, and twisted wire frames which must once have been supports for roses. Truly a garden is a fragile thing.

But there, in the middle, in full and glorious flower, was one of the loveliest yellow roses I have seen. The flower was full and quartered, the softest creamy-yellow and on a bush now at least two metres high and as many wide, the scent of the flowers heavy on the late afternoon air. My first thought was that this was 'Cloth of Gold'. But it was autumn, and 'Cloth of Gold' flowers only in the spring.

Louie was happy for me to take cuttings of it, and of the only other surviving rose, a cheerful cherry-red with Tea rose foliage, which was also in full flower on a bush the size of a small tree. This one, Louie said, gave her great joy as she was too old now to go into the garden, but could see it from the window.

The remains of paths were there, an ingenious twisted wire basket used to sup-port, I surmised, some sort of trailing plant, a weeping rose, perhaps. A wild tangle of Banksia rose and honeysuckle scrambled through two old apple trees and, under a twisted pear tree, was a huge patch of bright yellow *Sternbergia lutea*. I picked a big bunch to put in a bowl by the fire where Louie could see and enjoy them. She said there were still thousands of bulbs in the spring.

The next day I wrote to Louie, thanking her for her hospitality and for the rose cuttings. A week later came a letter from her. She had found the photographs and enclosed them with the letter.

They revealed a world long since gone – ladies in long dresses holding decora-tive parasols, the creator of the garden, proud and portly, with watch-chain and top hat. There were rose arches and arbours, paths edged in box or lavender (from the black and white photograph it was difficult to tell which). And here was the Gothic summerhouse, and roses looped along chains – and there in the middle what must have been my creamy-yellow rose. Here was formality indeed, in the midst of farming country in the very early days of Victoria. And somehow in no way incongruous.

My cuttings took and grew. Later I had knowledgeable visitors to the garden – Deane Ross and Walter Duncan, the big rose growers from South Australia – who both looked at my yellow rose and said, without hesitation, 'Cloth of Gold'. Now I have come upon several roses which are listed in English books as spring-flowering only, yet flower again for us, in our warmer climate, in autumn. Yet I have bought subsequently, from different growers, plants of 'Cloth of Gold' and they flower in spring only, while my rose from Camnethan continues to give a glorious display every autumn. So I call it simply 'Louie Wilson'.

I built my Gothic summerhouse in the paddock beyond the garden – but a summerhouse with a difference. I had it constructed as camouflage round an outdoor toilet and clothed it with the yellow 'Aviateur Blériot', pure white 'Silver Moon' and the creamy 'Albéric Barbier'. In front of them I planted a thick belt of shasta daisies (*Leucanthemum* × *superbum*).

Again we needed more topsoil. So, in the true Cathlaw tradition, we dug a second pond in a natural depression under the huge old pine tree at the back of the house. I wanted to line it in stone and for once I employed a self-styled 'expert' to do the job. He did a fine job, but I could not persuade him that a fountain would be out of place in a country garden (I had visions of rushing out, in French fashion, to turn it on every time a car drew up at the gate). So despite my emphatic rejection of the whole idea, he left a small hole in the stone floor – in case I should change my mind. In consequence of this the pond always leaked.

I planted the margins with *Iris kaempferi* (now *Iris ensata*, the Japanese water iris) in delicate shades of pink, blue and mauve, with white for contrast and deep purple for strength. They stood in water all the winter and we never watered them in summer and for me they were always the climax of the iris season, their great flat, saucer-shaped blooms coming, as they do, after the tall bearded iris are over. And on one corner I planted a huge clump of Maria's soft, tan-coloured *Iris louisiana*. Behind them I planted blue agapanthus to give colour in the summer months when the iris were over, and behind that again, inspired by Camnethan, roses on chains.

A trip to a demolition yard at Talbot – another of those forgotten little Central Victorian towns – yielded a good supply of beautiful old turned verandah posts. We used four of them here in a semicircle behind the pond and slung heavy chains between.

Rampant climbers would be out of place here – pillar roses were what was needed. On the outer two I planted the bright pink, almost thornless, recurrent-flowering Bourbon rose 'Zéphirine Drouhin', and on the inner two the softer pink, again almost thornless, recurrent 'Clair Matin'. Behind and between them I put the grey-leaved *Tanacetum ptarmiciflorum* syn. *Chrysanthemum ptarmiciflorum*. I had been given plants from a friend's garden and loved the grey foliage against the pink. The first year after I planted it I cut off all the flowers before they opened in order to preserve the compact shape of the bushes. I had assumed, also, that it

ABOVE: 'LOUIE WILSON'.

LEFT: 'CLAIR MATIN' AS A PILLAR ROSE WITH *TANACETUM PTARMICIFLORUM* AND *PYRUS SALICIFOLIA* AS A BACKGROUND TO 'NEWS'.

would be similar to *Tanacetum haradjanii* syn. *Chrysanthemum haradjanii*, which has an insignificant gaudy yellow flower which detracts greatly from the beauty of the grey foliage, and would quite ruin my pink and grey colour scheme. Fortunately I missed a piece and it delighted me with clusters of little white daisylike flowers.

Since then it has produced each year clouds of pure white blossom which are a perfect foil for the roses, especially for the soft pink of 'Clair Matin', and for the deep purples of 'Cardinal de Richelieu' and 'Hippolyte' nearby. It is frost-resistant and propagates relatively easily, though I never get a one hundred per cent strike, so I pot up replacement plants each year.

I was delighted with this corner of the garden and bought, in one of those 'antique' shops which have sprung up recently in every Australian country town, an old pine church pew – more at home in this country setting than scrolled iron work or classic teak. This was placed strategically under the old pine tree where one could sit, on summer afternoons, and watch the reflections of the iris in the water. And in the centre of the pond, on a moss-covered rock, I placed the little figure of a mermaid, shrouded in her own long hair, her hands clasped about her knees, the very essence of youth, and simplicity and gentleness. She was bought in a moment of reckless extravagance, the work of a sculptress friend of mine. The young model was Judith, my daughter's closest friend throughout her school days. She gives a focus and, for me, an added dimension to this corner of the garden, and is a constant source of joy.

SOME MODERN ROSES

A path was needed to link Little Portion to the main house for, due largely to my inability to envisage the final layout and design the garden on paper and all at once, the little cottage stood, initially, rather like the proverbial shag on a rock, with the Miniature Garden behind it and a broad expanse of what not even the most charitable of persons could call 'lawn' in front.

Lawn, I decided quite early in the piece, was an impossibility on the plains of Central Victoria. Pictures of those velvety emerald swards in English garden books filled me alternately with despair and envy. There was barely enough water for the garden, certainly none to maintain lawns through those terrible burning January and February days. Added to this, the seed from the paddock grasses was blown continually into the garden, so that we waged sporadic war with dock, dandelions, capeweed, thistles and sorrel, and the only green parts of the 'lawn' in summer were those where clover had taken a firm hold. I remember reading, with joy, an article by Tommy Garnett where he urged Australians to cease, in this respect, emulating English gardeners and to regard their lawns as annuals.

So when I decided to run a broad path, a generous path where two people could walk comfortably abreast, from the house to Little Portion I was not destroying an expanse of potentially beautiful lawn. I would love to have paved that path, which was forced to curve, as usual, round the moss-covered boulders, with old handmade bricks such as I had used in the Miniature Garden, but the expense was prohibitive, so in the end I settled for scoria. It looked cheerful against the sombre grey of the bluestone buildings and weathered, in time, to a warm rust colour.

I made wide beds on each side of the path, and, in the interests of having colour for as much of the year as possible and cut flowers for the house, I decided to opt here for some modern roses.

In choosing these I started from a position of abysmal ignorance. While I had read extensively about the old shrub roses I had totally neglected the enormously wide field of modern Hybrid Teas. Essentially what I wanted was some pink and white roses, with the occasional dark red, which would bloom without cessation from November till the end of May! What I ended up with was a collection of largely

ABOVE: MODERN ROSES IN A SHRUB
BORDER. 'DEAREST' IS TO THE LEFT OF
TANACETUM PTARMICIFLORUM WITH A
FOXGLOVE AND CHIVES IN THE FOREGROUND.

RIGHT: 'CLAIR MATIN' WITH FOXGLOVES.

1960s and 1970s roses including, as might be expected, a couple of inspired choices and some horrible mistakes.

There can be no gardener anywhere in the world who has not heard of 'Iceberg', 'the rose of the century'. Trouble-free, ever-blooming, long-lasting, it was my first choice among the whites, despite Peter Beales's rather scathing dismissal! 'Virgo' and 'Mount Shasta' were planted here and they are excellent, but in no way exciting. The really inspired choice among the whites was 'Swany'. The flower closely resembles that of 'Sea Foam' but, instead of growing tall, it forms a wide, procumbent shrub and it really does flower for months on end with a very minimum of attention beyond the cutting off of deadheads.

I have to confess to a soft spot for 'Queen Elizabeth'. I love her long, pointed buds and she is so tall that she is ideal at the back of a border where her awkward, ungainly legs can be hidden by lower growing perennials. My mother had grown 'Dainty Bess' when I was a child. I suppose she would be classed now as a 'nostalgia rose'. Certainly she is that for me. She produces her soft pink, single blooms with their striking reddish-brown stamens over a long period, although the bush is seldom robust. I was pleased, too, with 'First Love' and her offspring, 'Pink Parfait', a Floribunda in several shades of pink.

The most successful of the reds was undoubtedly 'Elmshorn', named after the first nursery established by that famous family of Kordes in 1887. As tall as 'Queen Elizabeth' it, too, is happy at the back of a border where it can be relied upon to produce its clusters of cherry-red blooms from spring until the end of autumn. The dark red 'Europeana' I found plain dull, and 'Eye Paint' and 'Old Master', two of Sam McGredy's 'hand-painted' roses, were certainly not for me. They performed well, and were striking and unusual so that they often attracted the attention of visitors to the garden, but to me they seem a crude and clumsy attempt to do what the old striped roses do so charmingly.

These roses were all planted on the north side of the path. On the south side, in an attempt to break the cold south wind, I planted five crab-apples. The few I had already planted had done better than any other trees with the exception of the birches. So, being on a good thing, I decided to stick to it. Especially as they had the additional qualification of belonging to the Rosaceae family. I chose two *Malus* 'Lemoinei' for the contrast of the dark, reddish-purple foliage and wine-red flowers, two *Malus spectabilis* – blush-pink flowers and little yellow apples – and the irresistible *Malus ioensis* 'Plena'.

Behind the crab-apples I planted a hedge of 'Stanwell Perpetual'. One day I shall amuse myself by making a list of the great roses which have started life as chance seedlings or sports. The list will be headed by this one and by the exquisite 'Souvenir de St Anne's'. There is a delightful story – the veracity of which I am not prepared to guarantee – that 'Stanwell Perpetual' was found as a seedling under a hedge in Somerset. Certain it is that most of the Spinosissimas (which many botanists prefer to call Pimpinellifolias), the Scotch Burnet roses, have vast numbers of little black hips and do set a vast amount of seed. 'Stanwell', however, sets no seed and is sterile. It is thought to be a cross between *R. spinosissima* and *R. damascena semperflorens*. We do know that it was released in 1838 by a nurseryman called Lee who had his nursery where London airport now is. Growing well over a metre high, it makes a sprawling shrub with grey-green, ferny foliage, and produces in spring and autumn great numbers of palest pink, flat, many-petalled flowers with a delicious scent. It needs little care and no pruning save for the removal of dead wood, and is sufficiently dense to make an ideal hedge.

Fascinated by the description, I planted beside Little Portion two or three plants of 'Wichmoss', released in 1911 and listed as a climbing Moss rose. Certainly the moss was plentiful, but I found the little cream flowers rather sparse and undistinguished and hardly worthy of the prominent place I had given it. The Miniature Garden was extended by the addition on the south side of a hedge of a dear little pink rose given me as cuttings by Nesta Mackellar.

High on a hill above the little township of Kyneton stands Woodside, one of the early bluestone homes which lend character to the district. Probably it had been built at about the same time as Bleak House, but by a rather more affluent person. The original owner, Captain Lavender, had come to Victoria from Maria Island off the coast of Tasmania, where he had been in charge of the penal settlement, and the property was known in the town as 'Lavender's old place', although Miss Mackellar had owned it for many years.

Approached by a long drive lined by dark old pines, it is surrounded by a rambling country garden separated from the farmland beyond by a hedge which had long since outgrown its allotted height and width. The old house, low and sprawling, its verandah clothed in climbing roses (now unpruned), was dignified still. High ceilings, french doors, marble fireplaces and cedar architraves lent an air of elegance which age could not detract from. Persian carpets, mahogany furniture, faded linen chair covers, solid family silver completed the picture.

And here Nesta Mackellar, in her late eighties, lived alone. And here she bred thoroughbred horses, racehorses, for which she cherished a passionate love, although she never had a bet on a race. On the south side of the garden was a gate in the hedge opening into the paddocks. There Nesta Mackellar had had a stone seat built where there was a view down to the Campaspe River and the Kyneton Racecourse beyond. Here she was sitting on the day I called about the roses, her binoculars in her hand, watching her horse, King Barak, on the track below. The race successfully over, we went round the garden.

The little pink rose must have been planted originally as a hedge round the kitchen garden. My cuttings took and made a hedge once more. It never grew above a metre in height and produced masses of small, mid-pink fragrant blooms, cup-shaped and borne in clusters – possibly it was one of the Poulsen roses, but I never had any confirmation of this, so called it simply 'Nesta Mackellar'. I never walk past it without thinking of that white-haired, dignified, independent old lady.

Having planted my modern roses, I addressed myself for the first time, seriously, to the question of spraying. This occupies a lengthy chapter in every book on rose growing, yet there are arguments against it. In the first place I had too many roses and not enough time to contemplate a regular spraying programme. In the second place I had a deep-rooted antipathy to filling the garden with poison every ten days or so. In the third place I was trying to encourage the birds. I would never persuade them that the garden was a haven for them if I regularly destroyed all the insects. So I made a firm resolution that, except in a dire emergency, I would not spray.

I had read a good deal about companion planting and about herbs, so resolved instead to underplant my modern roses (the old ones seem, with the exception of the Bourbons and the Hybrid Perpetuals, to be less susceptible) with herbs. It could certainly do no harm and might possibly do some good.

So I planted big clumps of chives *(Allium schoenoprasum)* – the cone-shaped mauve flower heads were ideal with pink roses – and spring onions. I had planted pink and white single hollyhocks near 'Queen Elizabeth'. The tall heads of garlic *(Allium sativum)* reached almost as high and created quite an architectural effect, reminding me always of the onion towers on the churches in the south of Germany. Garlic chives *(Allium tuberosum)* produced umbels of little white florets and scattered abundant seed – too abundant sometimes. Different thymes were used as groundcovers and the bulbs pushed up happily through the carpet they made. The enchanting blue-green lacy foliage of rue *(Ruta graveolens)* was perfect, but I tried always to cut off the acid-yellow flowers.

In my little cottage in Castlemaine with its pocket-handkerchief garden I had had a chamomile lawn. I had used the English chamomile*(Chamaemelum nobile* syn. *Anthemis nobilis)*. Hours of patient weeding were needed to establish it and anything so labour intensive was out of the question at Bleak House. But I did want to plant chamomile. Its reputation as an insect repellent made it a 'must' and its tiny white daisy-like flowers and fine feathery foliage made it ideal as a ground cover under roses. It thrived among the modern roses and almost reconciled me to 'Eye Paint' with its brilliant vermilion single flowers with their white eye.

I would love to have planted a rosemary hedge, partly for the scent, partly for the legends surrounding it, such as the one which claims that rosemary will never grow taller than the height of Christ. But I really had no place for any more hedges, so settled instead for planting rosemary in three big old coppers – one of the few things I grew successfully in tubs as it is so drought-resistant it does not mind if you forget to water it. I much prefer the pale misty blue flowers of the old rosemary *(Rosmarinus officinalis)* to the 'improved' variety, 'Blue Lagoon', with its much deeper blue. Prostrate rosemary *(R. officinalis* 'Prostratus') quickly formed an edging to some of the beds and spilled over on to the paths, softening the edges and scenting the garden when trodden on.

I had read that parsley is 'helpful to roses in the garden'. I am not sure in what way this helpfulness manifests itself, but certainly the crisp green of its curly leaves made it an excellent groundcover, especially under tall white roses.

Winter savory *(Satureja montana)* was tough, didn't mind the heat or the dryness, seeded itself quickly into the paths and went on happily year after year. And the bees simply loved it.

Borage *(Borago officinalis)* and feverfew *(Tanacetum parthenium* syn. *Chrysanthemum parthenium)* flourished and established colonies in all corners of the garden. For its name alone, I planted lady's bedstraw *(Galium verum)*, but it proved far too invasive and had to be removed – not without difficulty. I planted it instead under a vigorous contorted willow where it ramped away and quickly formed a large, soft mat, fit for any lady's bed on a hot summer's day.

How effective all this was in combating diseases of the rose I do not know. Whether useful or not, my herbs were beautiful. Certainly we suffered from black spot from time to time but never in plague proportions. Mildew was almost unknown to us and when friends from Melbourne were wringing their hands over plagues of thrip in the spring, we were relatively untroubled.

The birds came each year to the garden and nested there. Albert delighted me one Christmas when he appeared with a pretty little bird-feeder on a high post, which allowed us to feed them out of reach of the cats – and of Cara, whose favourite pastime it was to chase the magpies, although I am convinced that both she and they knew that she had no chance of success. Each year they nested in the huge old pine tree at the back of the house. I know of no lovelier sound than the call of the magpie on a spring morning. And I think they did a good job with the aphids.

The crab-apples on the south side were a huge success. They grew apace and were soon sufficiently sturdy for me to plant clematis to grow through them. They also set quantities of seed and I found little crab-apples coming up where they were least expected.

One came up in the middle of the path, just on the corner where it curved round the side of Little Portion. It was beautifully placed in front of two mossy boulders and a clump of white nerines. But as it grew larger, squeezing between it and the increasingly rampant 'Wichmoss' became a real problem. One or the other would have to go.

I was delighted one day by a visit from Jean Galbraith, botanist, lecturer, author and, above all, an inspired and impassioned gardener. As she pushed past the thorny arms of 'Wichmoss', stretched across the path, I apologised for the crab, explaining (quite unnecessarily) that it was a self-sown seedling and that I had been promising myself for months to move it.

'Why?' she demanded.

'It's in the middle of the path,' I said, stating the obvious.

'Well, then,' came the crisp reply, 'move the path!'

SOME EARLY TEA ROSES

uite early in my life as a rose gardener, I fell deeply and irrevocably in love with the early Tea roses. Most of them originated in France and, one and all, they have that air of elegance and sophistication we associate with things Parisian.

The first to be planted in the garden was 'Safrano'. He was first released in France in 1839, but the old cottage where I found him, rising out of a sea of thistles and dock, was a far cry from Paris. It was no more than a tumbledown shack made largely of galvanised iron and apparently held together by wire and pieces of baler twine. Across the back of the house, where once had been a verandah, was a large area enclosed by wire netting, an approximation to an aviary. In this were housed vast numbers of budgerigars and canaries. The old fellow who lived there sold them to eke out his existence. It stood in the midst of an old, overgrown garden – wild iris and daffodils, twisted old apple and pear trees, and across the front verandah, two metres high and as far across, was a fine bush of 'Safrano'. I did not know its name when I first found it, the late afternoon sun shining through its reddish foliage and lighting up the masses of blooms, the colour of rich dairy cream with just a hint of apricot.

The old chap was happy to give me cuttings – they were amongst my first successes, the result of much loving tender care. They rewarded me with a great profusion of bloom every spring and autumn. With a sense of nostalgia I paid a visit to the cottage recently, only to find it gone. The old fellow had won the lottery. With a desire, I suppose, to erase the memories of his former poverty, he had torn down the old cottage and built a brand new brick veneer. 'Safrano' was gone, and in its place was a row of standard 'Peace' and 'Blue Moon' on either side of the concrete front path. A hedge of photinia completed the picture, the old fruit trees having been consigned to the bonfire. Filled with sadness, I went home and, in protest, put in two large pots of cuttings of 'Safrano', my own bushes being by now large enough.

Gradually I added more Tea roses to the garden, although I found them more delicate than some of the others, and it needed care and constant vigilance to get them through our harsh winters.

I bought a simple soil-testing kit and found my soil to be slightly on the acid side of normal. I had suspected this from the steadily increasing stands of sorrel in the garden. So I bought large bags of lime and distributed it according to a regular timetable. This, together with twice-yearly applications of blood and bone with ten per cent of sulphate of potash added, gradually improved the soil. What there was of my topsoil was good and heavy but there was not a great deal of it. Albert built three huge compost bins out behind the barn and we religiously put all green weeds and vegetable matter from the kitchen into them. Rose prunings were burned and the ash added to the compost. All of this undoubtedly helped, but most effective, I think, were the truck loads of mulch I regularly collected from the racing stables in Kyneton.

Kyneton has a picturesque small racecourse and in its vicinity were two good trainers. The winters being so bleak, the horses are stabled on winter nights. The straw, with fresh manure, is swept out each morning, and the trainers were only too happy if someone came and carted it away. So I mulched, especially my Tea roses, with five to ten centimetres of straw and manure which the earthworms gradually carried down into the soil.

Ideal for a pillar or a pergola or on the verandah posts is the beautiful pure white 'Sombreuil', sometimes known as 'Mlle de Sombreuil'. Graham Thomas wrote of it that it is 'to be treasured for all time'. I certainly treasured mine and it repaid me by producing its wonderful, flat, very double blooms for months on end. Their perfectly heavenly scent on a spring morning is one of the glories of the garden. I grew it as a climber and gave it a pergola to climb over, but it never reached above two metres.

'Souvenir de Madame Léonie Viennot' was a horse of a different colour. Robust and vigorous, she attained a height of three metres in her first year and produced a mass of soft apricot double roses with copper tonings and a strong scent. The cuttings I took in her second year all struck with no need for the tender care I had lavished on 'Safrano'.

I planted three of 'Marie van Houtte', although *R. bracteata* later smothered one of them. She is a rich cream, heavily flushed with pink, and is generous with her very fragrant blooms, and sturdier than many of her relatives. She looks splendid with the little cream and pink eschscholzias as an underplanting. It does need constant vigilance to keep the dominant orange ones away and I found I had to pull them out regularly and throw them on the compost heap.

'Maman Cochet', again from France, and a daughter of 'Marie van Houtte', grows tall and angular but produces her slightly blowsy, untidy blooms in generous abundance. In the same bed I grew 'Baronne Henriette de Snoy'. I think I would have grown her for her name alone – how I wish I knew who the Baronne was. Her many virtues, however, rendered this piece of folly uncalled for. A daughter of that wonderful full, creamy-apricot 'Gloire de Dijon', she has all the virtues of her parent: full form, delicious perfume, frequent flowering. She does like a warm spot and rather resents heavy pruning, but is equally at home in the garden or in a large pot on a terrace. I grow her always with the soft pink violas round her feet, and she gives me infinite pleasure.

'Gloire de Dijon', herself a daughter of 'Souvenir de la Malmaison' is a 'must'. She does need support, as, with encouragement and a little pampering, she can be persuaded to reach a height of five metres.

With 'Général Galliéni', bred, again, in France in 1899 and named after the first Governor of Madagascar after it had become part of the French Empire, I had infinite trouble and no real success. He should have been a tough old fellow – his namesake is also reputed to have been responsible later for the defence of Paris at the beginning of World War I – but he resented the first hint of frost and, although I nursed him back to health each spring, he never really flourished. This was a bitter disappointment as I have seen him standing tall and sturdy in other gardens and I love his strange, irregularly shaped blooms, ranging in colour from buff, through various shades of pink, to deep red. I planted some of the old red and green alstroemeria with him and it throve as the Général languished. It had brought itself to the garden – another of Sarah Ann's legacies, perhaps – and I was somewhat alarmed to read later that, a native of South America, it so loves our climate that it has, in some places, escaped from gardens and taken on the nature of a weed. Certainly the yellow and orange varieties (*Alstroemeria aurea* syn. *A. aurantiaca*) grow wild on Mount Macedon, great sheets of gold and flame colour – perfectly splendid, but not beloved by the owners of the gardens.

It was while on holiday in Tasmania that I heard a romantic story of a red, red rose – reputedly an early Tea rose – the first rose ever to come to Tasmania. It had been brought out on a sailing ship from the famous old garden of Montacute in England to be planted in the garden of a grand old home built in the early days of the colony somewhere near Hollow Tree in central Tasmania, and named Montacute in memory of the owner's English home.

I could find no first-hand news of the old home, so set out one morning to look for it. We took the road which leads from Bothwell to Hamilton. Hollow Tree is no more than a name on a signpost. There was certainly no sign of Montacute, but there was an imposing old sandstone home overlooking the valley, so we drove in to make enquiries. In the big stone barn, Des Hallett was crutching sheep.

He was the fifth generation of his family to live in this home, and it transpired that he also owned Montacute. He told us how his great-uncle had bought it in 1905. He had driven to the auction in horse and buggy and arrived too late. So he offered the successful bidder $1000 and Montacute became his.

'There was a garden once,' Des Hallett said, 'but there's nothing now.' However, he gave us instructions. There is no road leading to Montacute and we had to drive across paddocks. The rough track seemed to go on for ever and we had opened and closed four gates and were quite sure that we had missed the way, when suddenly, high on a hill, we saw a church spire. Below it, in a valley, on the banks of a stream, lay Montacute.

The little church was well maintained, and all the headstones in the churchyard bore the name of Hallett, except for one right at the gate inscribed William Langdon.

The house was a different story. Quite deserted, shingles missing from the roof and the grand old fanlight over the panelled front door shattered, french doors standing open and the fine staircase dangerously broken, it spoke of loneliness and desolation. The remains of an orchard were there – huge pear trees and seedling apples and plums, and the foliage of what must have been a sea of daffodils in the spring – and the remnants of a high stone wall which surrounded the garden. Of roses there was no trace. Some of them are incredibly tough and resilient, so we searched all along the creek bank and through the long grass but could find nothing except for the little pink dog rose that grows wild all over Tasmania.

When I got home I searched for information about Montacute. It had been

'LADY HILLINGDON'
WITH *NEPETA* 'BLUE
HILLS GIANT'.

built, I discovered, in 1834 by Captain William Langdon. He was a sea captain, master of the *Lusitania* and prominent in the shipping world of early Tasmania.

He had been born in the Vicarage of Montacute in England, after which he named his new home. He took up two thousand two hundred hectares on the Clyde near Bothwell in 1823 and brought out between sixty and seventy persons from England. He imported stud cattle, horses, sheep and pigs, also deer and hunting dogs, pheasants and partridge. Birds for his aviary included the blackbird, thrush, goldfinch and skylark. He brought trees and shrubs, including a willow grown from a cutting taken from Napoleon's grave – and he brought roses.

The whole settlement was enclosed by a high sandstone wall. Blacks and bushrangers represented a constant threat. In 1855 William Langdon had built the little church and had it dedicated by the first Anglican Bishop of Tasmania.

Gertrude Jekyll, writing in 1904 of Montacute in England, said: 'Wonderful are those great stone houses of the early English Renaissance (it was built towards the end of the sixteenth century by Sir Edward Phelips) wonderful in their bold grasp and sudden assertion of new possibilities of domestic architecture.'

I wonder what she would have said of Montacute in Australia, this once charming and dignified home with its lovely gardens, its orchards and deer-park, set down in the midst of a strange and frightening land representing, with its little stone church, a tiny piece of the England William Langdon had known and loved. Wonderful, indeed.

It was a disappointment to find no roses at Montacute. We had no real clues to the identity of the rumoured red rose. The suggestion that it was an early Tea rose I did not take very seriously, for 'Adam' is usually accepted as the earliest of the Teas and he was bred in 1833. Most of them date from the end of the nineteenth century. It was more likely to have been an old Gallica.

We had taken a new road back to Ross and all thoughts of the red rose were driven abruptly from my mind when, round a bend, we came upon one of the most beautiful plants of 'Lady Hillingdon' that I have seen. At least two metres high and just as wide, she covered the wall of an old stone barn – a mass of golden roses. We got out to admire her. She has the same rich plum-coloured foliage as 'Safrano', lit up now by the setting sun. And her scent – a scent which Graham Thomas describes as 'the fragrance of a newly opened packet of tea with a hint of apricots' – filled the evening air. 'Lady Hillingdon' is one of the few early Teas which did not originate in France. She is English, bred by Lowe and Shawyer in 1910, the climbing form being a sport released in 1917. How warmly she must have been welcomed during those dark days of World War I!

Standing by the roadside I planned a new corner of the garden. Of course, she must be planted beside 'Safrano' and the underplanting must be blue: nepeta as basic ground cover; deepest blue Dutch iris for spring – I had a mental picture of them against the new red spring foliage of the roses – *Polemonium caeruleum* with its cup-shaped blue flowers and pretty leaves; the dwarf-growing electric-blue *Penstemon heterophyllus* and big clumps of what is, perhaps, my favourite among the geraniums, *Geranium himalayense*, which produces its violet-blue flowers all through the summer.

THE HYBRID MUSK
ROSES

enelope', 'Cornelia', 'Felicia', 'Thisbe', 'Moonlight' and 'Pax' – their very names conjure up pictures of old gardens, of Victorian times, of ladies in long skirts and picture hats, of portly old gentlemen with snowy beards and watchchains. Yet these roses are not so very old. They belong, most of them, to the first quarter of this century.

But they are a godsend to those of today's gardeners who have a leaning towards nostalgia and who want to plant 'old roses', but want them to flower more than once a year. They are just old enough to sneak into the old rose category and yet they have the capacity to flower not only abundantly but continuously.

The passion for 'old roses' was at its peak in this country in the 1970s, the Heritage Rose Society being founded, thanks to the untiring efforts of Trevor Nottle in South Australia, in 1978. Then, for a time, specialist rose nurseries were full of Gallicas, Damasks, Albas and Mosses. But the average Australian gardener – even the fortunate one – has only a quarter of an hectare or so at his disposal, and before long even those with an abiding passion for old roses were looking for a longer flowering period. It was then that the Hybrid Musks came into their own. Big, generous shrubs, most of them, up to two metres high and as much across, with subtle colours and strong perfume and, most importantly, the ability to flower for months on end – great trusses of flowers forty to sixty centimetres across and bearing fifteen to twenty individual heads of bloom.

What more could any gardener want? At about the same time cottage gardens came, very sensibly, into vogue. 'Very sensibly' because they fill the needs of the home gardener who wants colour and variety in his quarter of an hectare, and who loves to potter and experiment and plant seeds and take cuttings and whose home, in any case, would not lend itself to the setting of a formal garden. The Hybrid Musks are perfect for cottage gardens, for mixed borders, for growing with hollyhocks and penstemons, snapdragons and foxgloves, honeysuckle and paeonies.

I had planted six or seven 'Buff Beauties' and the same number of 'Penelope' along my western boundary fence before I was aware of the manifold virtues of the Hybrid Musks. But they had done all that I had expected of them and more.

They quickly outstripped 'Lamarque' (who hated our bleak winters) and 'Nevada' (who never looked really robust for me) and became the outstanding feature of that part of the garden. In the spring they covered themselves with glory and in the autumn the sight of 'Buff Beauty' against the russet, red and gold of the ornamental grapevine on the fence was quite unforgettable.

And then, one spring, I visited Heide, the sculpture park and garden at Bulleen, and realised that 'Penelope' was capable of even more than I asked of her. For here she was trained as a climber over a rose arch in the kitchen garden – and she was quite breathtaking.

A copy of *Rebels and Precursors*, given to me a few Christmases previously, had been my introduction to Heide and to John and Sunday Reed and the company of artists and writers they had gathered round them in an old, weatherboard farmhouse set in six hectares of paddocks which sloped down to the Yarra River near Heidelberg.

While John, with Sidney Nolan, Max Harris, Albert Tucker, Joy Hester and Arthur Boyd had painted and written, philosophised and argued, Sunday, brilliant, witty, elegant Sunday, who neither painted nor wrote, had created a garden. And this was, for her, and for the many people who visit it still, just another form of artistic expression.

With a total disregard for conventional and accepted concepts of garden design, she planted fruit trees, roses, vegetables and herbs in glorious profusion. Silverbeet grows amongst the wallflowers, lavender rubs shoulders with green peppers, zucchini vines trail among the roses.

And 'Penelope', on her rose arch, looks down on a tangle of soapwort, valerian, feverfew and mulleins. And further over, in the garden of the old house itself, she climbs, in company with wisteria, over a mellow brick wall.

Clearly the Hybrid Musks, vigorous and versatile, were worthy of far closer attention than I had, to date, given them.

They are one of the many legacies left to gardeners by the English clergy of Victorian times; times when the clergy had leisure to indulge in fox-hunting, quail-shooting, fly-fishing – and gardening.

All his life the Rev. Joseph Pemberton had loved roses. 'I was raised in a rose atmosphere and loved the rose when a child in petticoats,' he wrote. He grew up in a garden – the sort of garden where standard roses grew in a walled kitchen garden among the gooseberries and currants. He learnt to bud roses at the age of twelve. When taken to church on Sundays as a small boy he vied with the elderly gentleman in the next pew as to who had the finest rose in his buttonhole.

With his father, he regularly visited the rose shows at the Crystal Palace. And each November, when he went back to school, he took with him a flower of 'Souvenir de la Malmaison' in an empty barley sugar tin. This served as a constant reminder of home and all that it meant and it was taken home again, brown and battered from constant fingering, at Christmas time.

He started showing roses in 1875 and continued to do so for the next thirty years. In his retirement he devoted himself entirely to the breeding of roses.

In his very readable and scholarly book *Roses – their History, Development and Cultivation*, published in 1908, he devotes a chapter to hybridisation and cross-breeding. He lists the roses he found useful in his breeding programme – initially 'Trier' and 'Aglaia', both with *R. moschata* and *R. multiflora* in their parentage. He gives clear and detailed instructions for the amateur, would-be rose breeder, encouraging him to 'take it up seriously and he will find in it a recreation of deepest interest'. Certainly the Rev. Pemberton found in it both interest and success. There is little trace of the original Musk rose in his Hybrid Musks for he crossed his original parents with a succession of Teas, Hybrid Teas and Hybrid Perpetuals and, to use the words of Peter Beales 'he came up with a complete breakthrough – a distinct strain of long-flowering, shrub roses, with substantial flowers borne in clusters and in quantities equal to those of Polyanthas'.

Joseph Pemberton was inspired, perhaps, by his fellow cleric, the Rev. S. Reynolds Hole, Dean of Rochester. Inaugural President of the Royal National Rose Society, he is known to rosarians the world over. Kindly and genial, he found in gardening, and in roses in particular, his chief passion in life. He gives, in *The Six of Spades*, a delightful picture of the English country clergyman of the time:

> I cut a bouquet of the last roses of autumn ('Dijon's Glory', generous 'Jules Margottin', brave 'Maréchal Vaillant' and fair 'Souvenir de Malmaison') inter-mixing a few bits of hardy ferns and of feathers from the Pampas grass. After breakfast, writing a sermon with part of my posy before me ... I refreshed myself twice by peeping into my little houses, by a hasty survey of my treasures, in vinery, greenhouse and stove. For luncheon, I had a luscious, Beurré D'Amanlis pear, which I consolidated with a brace of dry biscuits, and medicated with a glass of sherry. In the afternoon I had a dig in my kitchen-garden, which made me feel as though I could swarm up the greasiest pole, and eat the leg of mutton afterwards; and then in my parochial walk I took two portions of the bouquet aforesaid, and two small bunches of grapes, to four of my sick folk; and I would that a certain earnest and eloquent London preacher, who told us that we clergy were not to entertain the desire of becoming good gardeners – I would that he had seen the smiles which welcomed both flowers and fruit.

Dean Hole planned and organised the first National Rose Show and travelled the length and breadth of England looking at gardens, talking to gardeners and encouraging local communities to establish their own flower shows. His first and most famous book, A *Book about Roses*, appeared in 1869. It was warmly received and widely read. So famous was he in his own time that when, on one occasion, he turned up unannounced to see the roses at Belvoir Castle, the home of the Duke of Rutland, the Head Gardener, when he learned the identity of his guest, so wished to honour him that he did the only thing that came to mind and shouted to the under-gardeners: 'Turn on the fountains, turn on the fountains!'

And there were, among the English clergy, others who left their mark and for whom roses became an abiding passion. There was Bishop Darlington, author himself of a book entitled simply *Roses* which appeared in 1911. One of the Hybrid Musks (but not one of Pemberton's) is named after him. And the Rev. Foster-Melliar wrote in 1910 *The Book of the Rose*. He was a great exhibitor and for him showing roses was more rewarding than breeding them.

Fortunately for posterity these men of the cloth considered rose growing, and gardening in general, as an occupation commensurate with their calling. The curate in Dean Hole's book, *The Six of Spades*, quotes, in justification of the time spent in his garden, the Book of Genesis, Chapter 2, Verse 8: 'And the Lord planted a garden eastward in Eden and there He put the man whom He had formed.' And he

concludes his dissertation on the joys of gardening with talk of 'the Christian gardeners who hear "the voice of the Lord God, walking in the garden"'.

So with heartfelt thanks to these clerics-cum-rosarians, I planted 'Bishop Darlington'. I put him in the same bed as 'Safrano', whom he somewhat resembles, being a semi-single of a most delicate creamy-apricot. 'Cornelia' and 'Felicia' are both of Pemberton's breeding. 'Cornelia' forms a big shrub, one and a half metres wide and just as high. She bears great heads of small apricot-pink blooms in splendid contrast to her bronze foliage. She looks fine beside the soft yellow of 'Buff Beauty' and with an under-planting of blue: *Veronica austriaca* syn. *Veronica teucrium* and *Veronica gentianoides*, whose leaves form a dense weed-suppressing mat; some of Fred's tall bearded iris; bog sage (*Salvia uliginosa*) with its sky-blue flowers and its tolerance of almost any garden conditions.

'Felicia' needs to be planted in a group of at least three and warrants a bed almost to herself. She was bred in 1928, the result of a cross between 'Trier' and the much-loved 'Ophelia'. She forms a bush something over a metre in height and breadth and bears soft, salmon-pink blooms continuously. I planted seven plants in a circular bed with the deeper apricot climber 'Souvenir de Madame Léonie Viennot' on a tripod as a centrepiece. For underplanting I used *Geum rivale* 'Leonard', the exquisite white sage (*Salvia staminea* syn. *Salvia transcaucasica*) and *Salvia sclarea* with its delicate white, mauve and pink-tinted flowers – an annual, this last one, but it sometimes sets seed and is, in any case, worth planting every year, for there is nothing like it for sheer delicacy of colour.

'Autumn Delight', not one of Pemberton's and of unknown parentage, became one of my favourites. Its semi-single flowers are the essence of simplicity – softest creamy-yellow, fading to white, with golden stamens. The foliage is a deep, polished green. In the same bed I planted 'Pax'. This is one of Pemberton's earliest and again bred from 'Trier'. It produces big clusters of pure white, nearly single blooms with amber stamens and it reaches a height of two metres. With Cathlaw in mind, I surrounded it with the scarlet *Geum* 'Mrs Bradshaw'.

'Vanity' I resisted for a number of years. It makes a big, sprawling, untidy bush with rather sparse foliage and I found its hot pink difficult to place. Finally, because of my ever-deepening affection for all its friends and relations, I succumbed and planted two together with an underplanting of blue, mauve and silver: the greyleaved *Tanacetum haradjanii* syn. *Chrysanthemum haradjanii* and blue violas at ground level, and *Campanula latiloba*, which blooms all summer through and sends its spires of lavender-blue blooms right up through the rose. It spreads quickly and forms a dense mat. And from Suzanne Price, who specialises in small and rare bulbs, I got bulbs of *Oxalis hirta* (small but not rare), which produces little open flowers like lavender jewels in autumn, is very hardy, multiplies quickly but is not at all invasive.

I remembered Christopher Lloyd and his six-metre hedge of 'Penelope', all struck from cuttings, and resolved to try propagating the Hybrid Musks myself as they really warrant planting in large groups. Without exception they struck easily and as I gloated over my little new plants as I potted them up I found myself thinking again of Dean Hole and his 'dear little cuttings, so bravely upright in their thumbpots; so charmingly conceited at having roots of their own!'

SPECIES ROSES IN THE ORCHARD

t the end of 1982 the farmer who had been agisting his sheep on my sixty-eight hectares decided he no longer needed the land, having bought another property adjoining his own. So I had to face the problem of what was to be done with this (to me) great expanse of grazing land. Ungrazed, it quickly becomes a bushfire hazard, so stock of some kind there had to be.

After much consideration I decided that the best solution was to build a small cottage and to put in a tenant who would, as a part-time occupation, look after the land, stocking it, either with his own sheep or mine. He might even be persuaded to lend a hand in the garden.

The cottage was built of stone from the property as Little Portion had been, and much thought was given to designing it in such a way that it would fit into the landscape and not be too much at variance with Bleak House itself. So well did we succeed in this that I had a visit one day, as the roof was going on, from Norm Ward from the big mill. He had just had an indignant phone call from a neighbour who had lived in the area all his life to say that 'the little old stone cottage north of Bleak House was being demolished and something should be done about it!'

We called it Satis, the name of Miss Haversham's house in *Great Expectations* – partly because I liked the idea of adding to the Dickensian flavour of the property, and partly because it was 'enough' – enough of building, enough of expansion, and in itself enough – no frills but cosy and comfortable – enough.

Between Satis and the end of the garden was one-third of a hectare of empty paddock. I did not want to extend the garden. The fence was already covered in ramblers. Trees, I decided, would form a pleasing link between the garden and the cottage. And, if trees, then why not fruit trees? And so an orchard was planned.

This was apple country and apples would obviously do well. Pears and plums were in all the old gardens in the area and I had seen big old walnut trees bearing heavy crops in Kyneton, eight and a half kilometres away. Apricots and peaches did not do well, but medlars did and quinces.

And so I planned an orchard on formal lines, with the trees in rows about six metres apart. I planted three varieties of pears and three of plums (I was especially attracted to one with the marvellous name of 'Sultan's Blood'!); walnuts and almonds, olives, quinces and medlars; one nectarine (as an experiment and because I love them, but it never fruited) and a great variety of apples.

In my choice of these last I was guided by my friend Ian Hargrave. Ian lived half an hour's drive north of Malmsbury at Harcourt in the granite belt, in the midst of Victoria's apple-growing district. Here he had a sixteen-hectare apple orchard, an enchanting old granite house built by his grandfather, a rambling country garden and a small nursery. Peacocks and pheasants roamed the garden; the most prolific 'Nancy Hayward' rose I have ever seen adorned the front verandah; and in a small outbuilding, now a gallery, hung a collection of Ian's watercolours. He loved this part of Victoria and he painted the early settlers' cottages, the old pubs and barns of the district – many of them now demolished. In the intervals between painting, collecting antiques and playing the very beautiful old harpsichord before the open fire in his living room, he gardened.

On his advice I planted Jonathans, Red Delicious, Golden Delicious, Stewart's Seedling, Five Crowns, Cox's Orange Pippin, and, from Clive Winmill at Badger's Keep, one with the inexplicable name of 'Winter Banana'.

Right on the fence-line, after a great deal of thought and with many misgivings, I planted a row of the Leyland cypress (× *Cupressocyparis leylandii*) to form both a windbreak and a visual break.

I had decided not to prune my fruit trees except for the removal of old wood and badly crossing branches. I could never possibly use a fraction of the fruit they, when mature, would produce. Blossom and fine-looking trees were my objective.

Just at this time a friend, seeing my young orchard, presented me with half a dozen Chinese silky chickens and half a dozen ducks – beautiful ducks they were, with bronze feathers and deep turquoise-green heads. They would add a splendid touch, free-ranging among the trees.

The very first night we lost one to a marauding fox who had crossed the paddocks from the quarries. Willy was obviously not taking his duties as a watchdog seriously enough, so both chickens and ducks would have to be shut up at night. Henhouses are traditionally unlovely things and I was loath to spoil the appearance of my orchard. After lengthy consultation with Albert, I decided we would have two A-frame houses, painted charcoal grey and planted with the climbing rose 'Paul's Scarlet', one for the hens, one for the ducks. Albert set to work with a will and by nightfall the first one was up and painted. Enticed by a handful of wheat, the ducks went in happily and seemed to accept this as home.

I was reminded again of Cathlaw as we dug the pond for them. But we wanted water this time, not topsoil. It was a good-sized pond. We lined it with plastic and Albert and I paved it with flat stone from the quarries, set in cement. With the cement we mixed a waterproofing compound and dark grey colouring matter and were well pleased with the result. The margins were planted thickly with blue agapanthus and yellow cannas and a couple of big clumps of pampas grass which would provide shelter for the ducks and a nesting place should the spirit move them. This done, we filled the pond with water and stood back and watched with great satisfaction as the enthusiastic ducks took their first swim.

I was very taken that spring with *Rosa canina*, the little pale pink dog rose which grows wild in the quarries. The birds had dropped seed in the garden, too, and it came up in unwanted places. Despite its delicate flowers and colourful hips, it is really not for the garden, being a thorny, awkward, tangled shrub, and yet I wanted it somewhere (other than in the quarries), both for its beauty and for its historic significance, it being the commonest of the wild roses native to Britain and Europe.

So I dug a couple of seedlings out of the garden and planted them in the orchard. And this was the beginning of a collection of species roses. I had left a generous space between trees, so decided to plant a row of species roses between each two rows of trees, so that I had roses and trees alternately. Here it would not matter if they grew large and untidy. There would be no need to prune them and they could grow as they would do in the wild.

So began a new love affair. There is something very appealing about the species roses – the freshness and simplicity of the small, single blooms, and the thought that they are today as they have been for many thousands of years, long before the birth of Christ. Many of them have colourful hips, some of them beautiful foliage and some of them wonderful autumn colour. They originated in Britain, in Europe, in the USA and Canada, in Asia and in the Middle East. Strange that none of them is native to the southern hemisphere, and yet they are quite at home when planted here.

I chose with care, but my choice was, by necessity, limited by commerical availability. At the top of my list was *R. willmottiae* from western China. I had never seen it growing, but had read descriptions of its fine, bluish-tinted foliage, plum-purple stems and small lilac-pink flowers. More importantly, I had just finished reading Audrey le Lievre's *Miss Willmott of Warley Place*, a fascinating account of the life of that inspired and eccentric gardener for whom the rose was named when it was brought to England in 1904. I have only once handled a copy of her great book, *The Genus Rosa*, the culmination of her life's work, but some of the wonderfully detailed watercolours which she commissioned Alfred Parsons to paint were made available to us again in 1987 by Graham Stuart Thomas in his book *A Garden of Roses*.

Next came *Rosa farreri persetosa*, again from China, chosen partly for its name, the Threepenny Bit Rose, and partly because of a picture I had seen of the long arching canes weighed down with tiny, mauve-pink flowers. Since for newer generations of gardeners a 'threepenny bit' is no longer a concept, I expect this delightful name will fall into disuse. 'The One-cent Rose' does not have the same charm!

It was some of the American roses which provided spectacular autumn colour in the orchard. *Rosa setigera* (the Prairie Rose), which has its origins in the USA and in Canada, forms a big sprawling bush with cerise-pink fragrant blooms and fewer thorns than most. *Rosa woodsii fendleri* has attractive ferny foliage, lilac-pink flowers with soft golden stamens, followed by clusters of red hips. And, most spectacular of them all, *Rosa virginiana* with red-tinted stems, bright pink flowers with yellow stamens and autumn foliage that turns from gold to flame red, to orange, to purple and every shade in between.

Rosa sweginzowii from north-west China I chose for its hips – orange-red, shaped like little flagons, comparable only with those of *Rosa moyesii* and its hybrids.

Rosa glauca, which when I planted it was known as '*Rosa rubrifolia*', is the landscape architect and flower arranger's dream – not for its flowers, which are the usual lilac-pink and quite undistinguished, but for the wonderful purplish colour of its stems, its bluish-grey foliage and its spectacular hips. At a distance, in autumn it resembles quite strikingly *Crataegus tanacetifolia* (also, of course, a member of the Rosaceae family).

I think it was the thorns which earned *Rosa sericea* var. *pteracantha* a place in the collection. As it comes from Mount Omei in China it was known for a long time as

R. omeiensis pteracantha. Much easier are its popular names, the Wing-thorn Rose or the Maltese Cross Rose – the latter because it is a rarity in having only four petals. The tiny pure white roses are delightful, but the thorns are the real feature – huge, elongated and blood-red, they make it a formidable bush. It is best planted where it will catch the rays of the setting sun.

Two shorter, suckering, thicketing roses, both from North America and Canada, form great decorative clumps. *Rosa blanda* produces pink flowers, larger than most of the species roses, and it is almost thornless. *Rosa nitida* is another of those with glorious autumn colouring. Its bright pink flowers are followed by round red hips.

I planted two great climbers in the orchard, but since there was nothing for them to climb on in that flat expanse they just formed great, sprawling mounds. *Rosa brunonii* (the Himalayan Musk Rose) will climb twelve to fifteen metres up trees, where its clusters of little white fragrant blooms, admirably set off by its grey-green foliage, hang down in great festoons. Alas, there was no opportunity for such a display here, but it performed admirably nevertheless. *Rosa moschata*, with its haunting, musky scent, flowered in early summer and often again in autumn. Coming from southern Europe and the Middle East, perhaps it was more at home in Australia than in the colder climate of England, where it first made its appearance during the reign of Henry VIII.

No collection of species roses would be complete without at least one of the pale yellow ones from China. So I planted *R. hugonis*, brought to Europe in 1900 by Father Hugh, a French missionary. The ferny foliage sets off the tiny, soft buttercup-yellow flowers, which are followed later by rather inconspicuous reddish-black hips. *R. primula*, also from northern China and Turkestan, has long arching canes, set with creamy-yellow flowers. The foliage is said to carry the scent of incense, hence its popular name, the Incense Rose. I cannot honestly say I have noticed it.

I have left *R. eglanteria* till last – eglantine, the sweet briar of England, sung by Shakespeare, conjuring up memories of English hedgerows and country byways. Its bright pink roses in clusters are followed by brilliant scarlet hips which hang on into the winter, and the foliage, when crushed, has a scent of apples – so much so that at Mottisfont Abbey, the great rose garden planned by Graham Stuart Thomas in the early 1970s, *R. eglanteria* is planted behind the seats around the fountain which forms the centrepiece of the garden so that 'whichever way the wind blows, the sweet apple aroma will reach the seated occupants'.

So the orchard became much more than a collection of fruit trees. Here were gathered together roses from far-flung corners of the globe and from times far distant from our own.

Many of these big sprawling bushes with their fine foliage and tiny single blooms bear little resemblance to their descendants, the roses of today. For Australians this has a special importance. We have no species roses of our own but where modern roses with their often opulent flowers look ill-at-ease with our Australian native plants, these old species roses look at home. They open up new possibilities for gardeners who have devoted themselves mainly to Australian natives and have thought that, for them, roses were out of the question.

The Chinese silkies and the ducks flourished. At one stage the duck population reached thirty! They never did nest under the pampas grass provided for them, but preferred instead the inner recesses of the mounds of *R. moschata* and *R. brunonii* or the honeysuckle we had planted along the orchard side of the fence to mingle with the rambling roses on the garden side.

MY INTRODUCTION TO ALISTER CLARK

t was some time in early 1983 – just after I had retired in Melbourne and was revelling in being able to work full-time at Bleak House – that I had a momentous visit from Tommy Garnett.

We had met briefly some ten years earlier, when we were both involved in education, but since then, although I was a regular reader of his wide-ranging articles in the weekly gardening supplement in the *Age*, Melbourne's leading daily newspaper, I had had no personal contact with him.

I had visited his fascinating garden at Blackwood, The Garden of St Erth, started when he was still Headmaster of Geelong Grammar School, and carried on with legendary vigour, enthusiasm and botanical knowledge in his retirement. A real plantsman's garden, this one, extending over some four hectares deep in the Wombat Forest. As well as a European garden, with an extensive collection of exotic plants, all meticulously labelled, there are informal Australian gardens where native plants grow in the bushland setting which they love. There are roses and clematis, an orchard, and a kitchen garden which supports the entire extended family, an alpine garden, a herb garden, a section devoted to iris and one to sorbus, a rare collection of cistus – Tommy's interests in the plant kingdom are extensive indeed and his knowledge encyclopaedic.

He had been interested, he said, in what I had been doing at Bleak House and had come to have a look for himself and to talk to me about Alister Clark, about whom he was writing a book.

I find it hard now to credit, following eight years of reading and searching, after immersing myself in his diaries and articles, that at that time his name meant nothing to me. Tommy, however, was not surprised. It meant nothing to most Australians. And yet Alister Clark was the greatest rose breeder this country has ever known – the only one to have won international acclaim.

He was born at Bulla, on the outskirts of Melbourne, in a wonderful old home called Glenara, painted by Von Guérard, classified by the National Trust and listed on the Historic Buildings Register. And it was here, after being educated in England and Scotland and later at Cambridge, that he lived for most of his life. His interests were wide and, since although he studied law he never practised, he had leisure to pursue them. His marriage certificate, when he married Edith Rhodes in New Zealand, listed his profession simply as 'gentleman'.

THE HOUSE AT
GLENARA WITH *R.
BANKSIAE* 'LUTEA',
WISTERIA AND
'CRAMOISI
SUPÉRIEUR'.

He was a fine horseman. There are many photographs in the family archives of Alister in riding or hunting gear. His diaries in the earlier years speak of hunt meetings when he was Master of the Hunt, of polo matches and the ponies he regularly brought from New Zealand after holidays spent there with Edie. He owned and bred racehorses and was founding President of the Moonee Valley Race Club. His portrait hangs in the Committee Room to this day and the Alister Clark Stakes is run each year in the spring.

He was a keen golfer, a foundation member of Royal Melbourne, and his diary entries tell frequently of trips to Cranbourne to play golf with his great friend Albert Nash on his private golf course. After a morning's golf he frequently returned to Glenara to spend the afternoon ferreting – rabbits were always a problem. He was a fly-fisherman and an excellent amateur photographer, as photographs of his in the family collection testify. He had a keen social conscience and was a Justice of the Peace and served on the local Council. He was one of the first to grow grapes for wine in this part of Victoria.

But what was of greatest importance to me – and perhaps to Alister himself – was that he maintained and extended the fine garden started in his father's time and there he bred daffodils and some one hundred and thirty-five roses – many of them bred especially to suit Australian conditions.

Glenara lies in a gully, protected and warm, and Alister embarked on his career as a breeder of roses with a specific object in mind. He wanted to breed roses which would flower throughout the year. He had observed which roses did best in the mild climates of the Mediterranean and Ireland, and he had nurserymen scour Europe for the roses listed by the great English gardener William Robinson as the best garden roses.

This is important, for Alister was interested in producing not prize exhibition blooms but roses which would do well in the garden, what he called 'decorative roses'.

Unfortunately for rosarians, the book in which he kept records of his breeding programme was left out in the rain one night towards the end of his long life and ruined, so the parentage of many of his roses remains unknown. We do know, however, that he used extensively the great vigorous white climber *Rosa gigantea*, from Burma and the Himalayas, which, under favourable conditions, will climb to a height of twelve metres. At the time this was a breakthrough. Horace McFarland, president of the American Rose Society, writing of Alister Clark says: 'Only in Australia has the rampant *Rosa gigantea* proved amenable to the hybridizer, so that its progeny get into commerce.'

Using *Rosa gigantea* Alister produced vigorous climbers, many of which bloomed very early. Best known is, perhaps, 'Jessie Clark', named after his niece and, of course, a second-generation *gigantea* hybrid, 'Lorraine Lee'. This last-named flowers so prolifically that W. H. Dunnallan, writing in the *Rose Annual* of 1932 could say that a bunch of 'Lorraine Lee' was shown at every meeting of the National Rose Society for twenty consecutive months.

It is easy to see why such a rose took Australia by storm. Hedges of 'Lorraine Lee' were planted all over Melbourne and Adelaide. E. W. Hackett, a South Australian nurseryman, wrote in his 1934 Catalogue that in the ten years from 1924–34 his nursery sold 44,000 plants of 'Lorraine Lee'. (One is tempted to draw parallels with 'Iceberg' today!) And not only is it prodigal of its blooms, but it is one of the most beautifully scented of all roses, and hardy to boot. Alister himself wrote in the *Rose Annual* of 1931: 'May I plead with those who grow "Lorraine Lee" not to overfeed or overprune it. I find it does wonderfully at Glenara if practically left alone.'

The *Annual* of 1938 speaks of a plebiscite held through the columns of the *Argus*, a now defunct Melbourne daily, which resulted in a triumph for Alister Clark, for his rose 'Lorraine Lee' headed the list. It was described as 'the most popular rose ever introduced in Australia'.

Much later I had a delightful letter from Wendy Langton, the proprietor of that invaluable antiquarian bookshop in Adelaide which specialised in garden books. She wrote:

> In 1941 my mother saved up nine shillings out of her housekeeping money and sent my brother, then aged nine, with his billy-cart around to the local nursery-man to bring home twelve 'Lorraine Lee' roses. These she planted as a hedge along the front fence and, as you can imagine, my memories of childhood home-comings are always fragrance-filled as a result.

Now none of this was known to me on the day of Tommy's visit. I had heard of 'Lorraine Lee' and of 'Black Boy', but the name of their breeder was unknown to me. However, I was ready for a new project and Tommy is persuasive, his enthusiasm infectious, so that when he said, 'I am writing about Alister's life. Why don't you collect the roses?' I agreed to do so.

Little did I appreciate the difficulties I would encounter. Nor did I realise that this would occupy a good deal of my time over the next ten years, and that the chances of finding more than a fraction of them were slim indeed.

In the first place, the people who knew him as adults were now mostly over eighty. In the second place, there are no real records. Alister's book was lost so the only sources of information, apart from sometimes unreliable memories, are early Australian rose books, the *Annuals* of the Rose Society and early nursery catalogues. Most of the descriptions are scanty in the extreme: '"Bright Boy" – dazzling red blooms, tall vigorous grower' (Hazelwood's Catalogue, 1941). How many red roses would fit this description!

Photographs taken at the time are mostly of poor quality and nearly all black and white, so are of little help in identification. All but 'Lorraine Lee', 'Black Boy' and 'Nancy Hayward' had entirely vanished from nurserymen's lists. Nearly fifty years had elapsed since Alister's death. No one had any commercial interest in promoting his roses. Gardens change. Properties change hands. Old roses are rooted out and new ones planted.

I made a start, however, without delay. My first step was to invite Nancy Hayward to lunch. Fortunately, she is my husband's aunt, so when she visited Melbourne from Adelaide it was not difficult to persuade her to come to Bleak House. With the best of intentions I made a rushed trip to Atherstone, Ian Hargrave's nursery at Harcourt, and brought back a large bunch of 'Nancy Hayward' roses. These I arranged with care in a beautiful old vase which had belonged to my mother and put them on the lunch table.

Aunt Nan duly arrived and was ushered into the dining room. I waited expectantly for her cries of delight. Instead she exclaimed: 'I can't stand that rose! Alister never asked me if he could name it after me. It has too few petals, no scent, and is a perfectly horrible colour!' There was nothing for it but to remove them hastily to the kitchen. We were not off to a good start.

Sadly, she could tell me little of Alister. Her father, Sir William Irvine, had been Patron or Vice-Patron of the Rose Society every year from 1928, when the Australian

Rose Annual was first published, until his death in 1943, so he must have known Alister well. But the family saw little of him and Aunt Nan's recollections were hazy.

My second step was to pay another visit to Eve Murray at Langley Vale. Tommy had told me that she and Alister had been good friends. The fact that they were both daffodil breeders had given them a great mutual interest.

It was a still, sunny March afternoon and as I pushed open the garden gate at Langley Vale I saw Eve in her wheelchair on the back verandah. With a large barrow of daffodil bulbs on one side of her chair and a barrow of pots and potting mix on the other side, she was potting up daffodils for sale at her next Open Day in aid of the Kyneton Hospital.

She was delighted to help and full of stories about Alister. Her eyes lit up as she talked of him and of the daffodil shows they had both attended and of old Hugh Dettman, Alister's friend and rival, who had lived in Kyneton.

Down at the bottom of the garden at the foot of a steep slope she had a collection of Alister's roses. With great skill and much laughter she manoeuvred her chair down the winding paths. She was only too happy for me to take cuttings, happy that the roses were not to be irretrievably lost. Here I found 'Ringlet', a fairly vigorous climber bearing great clusters of single pink and white blooms. Here also was 'Sunny South'. Much later, when I came to read the old *Rose Annuals,* I found that Alister himself had written of it: '"Sunny South" is my favourite of all the seedlings and imported roses that I have tried out in the last sixty years or so.' W. H. Dunnallan thought it should have become Australia's national flower. He wrote in 1931:

> On a visit to a country town last week I came across 'Sunny South' growing in
> almost every garden, and in many places where there was no garden it flourishes
> amazingly without attention. I came upon a hedge of it a hundred yards long and
> a mass of bloom … It can surely be said that Mr Clark has raised a universal Rose.

'Editor Stewart' was here, a splendid large vibrant cherry red Pillar rose with wavy petals and beautiful young red foliage. It was named after Alister's great friend who was for many years editor of the *Rose Annual.* Alister rejected a number of seedlings until he found one he thought worthy to carry his friend's name.

And here, too, was 'Fairlie Rede', a beautifully formed, fragrant, soft silvery pink. And 'Diana Allen', described in Hazelwood's Catalogue of 1941 as having blooms resembling small carnations. And 'Sunlit', which found its way to the USA. It produces in great profusion small blooms of softest apricot. It was illustrated in colour in the American *Rose Annual* of 1943 and described as being 'a rose worthy of a place in anyone's garden'.

Eve pointed out another tall bush covered in classic-shaped blooms of soft pink. 'He gave me that one to try out,' she said. 'He often gave seedlings to his friends. Sometimes he registered them later and sometimes he thought they weren't good enough. He died before the fate of that one was decided.' So I took cuttings of it, as well as of all the others, and when it grew and flowered we called it simply 'Mrs Murray's Seedling'.

There was a large, low bush, simply covered with clusters of the most cheerful bright pink flowers. 'That's "Cherub",' said Eve. 'Alister loved it.' From the cuttings of 'Cherub' I had a hundred per cent strike and when it bloomed in the garden at

Bleak House the following year everyone loved it. But by then I had gleaned more scraps of information about Alister's roses and 'Cherub' was described in 1923 by Brundrett, who marketed it, as 'a very vigorous climber with profuse, non-recurrent bloom'. Clearly this was not the low-growing, tireless performer I had got from Eve.

I put it on 'hold', pending more information. But in the meantime it was in constant demand since it flowered incessantly. Finally I persuaded John Nieuwesteeg to propagate it for me and we called it simply 'Not Cherub'!

Later on the afternoon of that visit as we sat on the verandah and drank tea, Eve reminisced about Alister, about the magic of the garden at Glenara, about his energy and drive, about the little dogs Edie, his wife, always kept, about the huge bowls of roses he took to every Rose Show, although he himself was not an exhibitor, and about his kindness to everyone he came in contact with. She told me how once, when she and Alister were driving together through Canterbury, he suddenly stopped the car and rushed into a house to ask directions. The woman who answered the door came out to show him the way and, inevitably, they walked around her garden discussing her roses. When he got back into the car Eve asked him why on earth he had asked directions when he knew perfectly well the way to go. 'Well,' he said, 'there was the most marvellous rose in the garden and I had to see it somehow!'

Little did I realise, as I drove home that evening, that this was the biggest collection of Alister Clark roses I was ever to find in one garden. Many subsequent searches ended in a blank, often after weeks of looking and many miles travelled. At most I might find one and that came to be cause of great rejoicing.

But with the institution of this search Bleak House had gained a purpose, something outside and larger than itself. If the garden was good enough and the search for the lost Alister Clark roses was successful enough, it might serve to reinstate in the minds and gardens of Australia this man who had devoted much of his life to the breeding of roses for Australian conditions, who won recognition and acclaim in America and in Europe and who had, to our shame, been forgotten here.

For Alister Clark was recognised not only in his own country. His roses were planted in the great rose garden at Bagatelle in Paris and at Sangerhausen in Germany. He was the first Australian to win the coveted Dean Hole Medal for service to the Rose (there have only ever been two others, the late Dr A. S. Thomas and Mr David Ruston). He was awarded Honorary Life Membership of the American Rose Society in 1931; in Britain, he was elected Vice-President of the Royal Horticultural Society in 1944, an election which was described as a 'well-deserved recognition of a great horticulturist which is also a signal honour to Australia'. And when, on the death of T. A. Stewart, an award was instituted 'to be made at suitable intervals to those in Australia and New Zealand who have given outstanding service in the interests of the Rose' Alister Clark was the first recipient. To regain for this great Australian some measure of recognition in his own land was an objective worth striving for.

GLENARA

On Alister Clark's death, such was the esteem in which he was held, it was decided to establish an Alister Clark Memorial Garden at the St Kilda Botanical Gardens in Blessington Street. The garden was to contain a percentage of his roses but also imported roses. Donations came from Rose Societies all over Australia, for his name had become almost synonymous with the Rose. The garden was opened (significantly, perhaps?) on a wet day in the presence of his widow, and it was felt to be a fitting tribute to a great horticulturist.

Having read of this, I set out one morning to visit the garden, sure that here I would find some more of the roses. I found the St Kilda Botanical Gardens, in Blessington Street, without difficulty, but it proved to be a bitter disappointment. Forty years had elapsed since Alister's death and the Memorial Garden was a tangle of dead and ailing rose bushes, broken trellis and weeds. The only identifiable roses (name tags were broken, misplaced or missing altogether) was 'Black Boy', struggling on manfully and, of course, the ubiquitous 'Lorraine Lee'. I could only assume that, when the Garden was established, no financial provision was made for its upkeep.

Disappointed, I returned home, filled with bitter thoughts about the shortness of people's memories, the transitory nature of all earthly things and other such profundities. Determined to rid myself of such unproductive ideas, I decided to make contact with Glenara itself.

On Alister's death an attempt had been made (in the absence of any children) to acquire Glenara for the nation. This came to nothing and the property had passed into private hands. The new owner cared nothing for all that Glenara stood for. Presumably his interest was in the acquisition of broad acres so close to the city of Melbourne. So oblivious was he of the garden and its place in Australia's history that he even let stock in to eat part of it down. Fortunately, his tenure was short and Glenara passed then to a Melbourne solicitor and his wife, Eric and Ruth Rundle. Their main interest lay in horses rather than in gardens, and they took over where Alister left off at the Oaklands Hunt Club, one of their daughters being subsequently the Master of the Hunt. But they were conscious of the beauty of the home and it has been meticulously preserved. So anxious is Ruth Rundle to retain the atmosphere of Glenara that some of Alister and Edie's curtains have been hung again in the house, and Alister's portrait hangs in the entrance hall.

I resolved to make contact with Ruth. Her husband had been killed not many months earlier in a hunting accident and she was living alone at Glenara. Tommy had recently been to see her about his book and experts from the Royal Botanic Gardens, Melbourne, had come to look at some of the rare trees that Alister's father, Walter, had planted in the garden. Now I came, wanting to look at the roses. After thirty-odd years of quiet possession of the property which had become their home, it must have been bewildering and sometimes more than a little annoying to have so much semi-public interest taken in it.

But Ruth Rundle was courteous and generous in the extreme. She listened to what I had to say, invited me to visit Glenara and to take what rose cuttings I wanted. Naturally she was worried about the state of the garden and apprehensive about people's reaction to it. When Alister lived there he had employed anything up to eight gardeners. Ruth Rundle had none – only a man to help with the mowing and someone who came in once a year to do a bit of pruning.

My sister from Queensland was holidaying with me and together we set out one still April afternoon for Glenara. It was with feelings of excitement and anticipation that I turned off the Bulla Road and into the gates of Glenara. There is nothing to be seen from the road. The gates are unremarkable and the drive leads through horse paddocks until it curves sharply and drops into the valley. Then through a gap in the hedge on the left-hand side of the drive the first roses come into view and one enters a magical world.

We parked on the gravel drive in front of the grand old home. The little red China rose, 'Cramoisi Supérieur', was in full flower on the verandah and in my imagination I saw it with the little yellow Banksia rose and the wisteria which were planted there also in flower. The gardens slope down from the house to Deep Creek and in Alister's day these slopes were thickly planted with roses. The stones outlining what were once beds are still in place and the surviving roses give some idea of what must once have been. Many of them were in the full flush of their autumn bloom on bushes the size of small fruit trees, climbing roses reaching up into the branches of trees, huge bushes of roses mounded together and supporting each other, filling the air with fragrance – and some poor little bushes ravaged by drought and wallabies and rabbits, but still putting on a brave show, such is the tenacity of the rose.

A picturesque wooden bridge leads across the creek, and the ground rises steeply on the other side, crisscrossed with winding paths which take one to the very romantic stone watchtower on the hill opposite the house. This was all once part of the garden. Now the only surviving plants are some cacti and a mass of seedling eucalypts. These slopes were once a carpet of daffodils, some of which still struggle through today.

Going down from the house to the right, winding paths lead through trees, a mass of smilax and periwinkle and a forest of agapanthus to great granite boulders overlooking the creek, and steps which had been cut in the rock leading down to the water. Here sweet peas still push their way up through the long grass and the daffodils are thicker.

In front of the winery and in the vegetable gardens where Alister had also put his untried seedlings are huge impenetrable mounds of roses, and everywhere stone edgings and carefully made steps speak of past glories.

Nostalgia was in the air, and romance – nothing of the atmosphere of depression and decay which had surrounded the garden at St Kilda. We both felt excited, and very privileged to be there and I found myself more determined with every moment to find again the roses bred in this beautiful place.

I had brought secateurs, a quantity of newspaper and a pile of plastic supermarket bags and we set to work. I took cuttings from sixty-four different bushes and, while I cut, Jennifer wrapped each bundle in wet newspaper and tied it in a plastic bag and numbered the bags Glenara 1-64.

How we were ever to identify them was a problem I did not want to contemplate. For the present my only thought was to preserve as many as possible before the rabbits or the wallabies or a future drought should do away with them altogether.

There were no garden records. There were no name tags or plans of the garden. Alister had grown roses other than his own so there was no certainty that the cuttings we took were even from his own roses. We put all these thoughts from our minds and worked steadily on till approaching darkness put an end to it.

It was quite dark when we got back to Bleak House, but the cuttings had to be potted up that night. Any delay decreases the chance of success.

My sister (who is not a gardener) was appalled at the prospect. While I searched in the shed (which had no light) for plastic pots and propagating mix (which fortunately I mixed in large quantities so that it would always be readily available) she slipped down to Malmsbury and came back with a cask of Lindeman's Claret.

'If we're going to be here until midnight,' she said firmly, 'we're going to enjoy ourselves.' So she stoked up the fire, put on a recording of Scott Joplin, got out the glasses and we set to work.

By midnight some two hundred and sixty little cuttings were safely in their pots. A good proportion of them struck. Many of the climbers did not. Those bred from *Rosa gigantea* stock are notoriously difficult to propagate. Some of them we were later able to identify. Some are still known simply as 'Alister Clark's Pink Floribunda', or 'Alister Clark's Cream' or 'Alister Clark, NOT Tonner's Fancy'.

Having got so far, I was at a loss as to how to proceed next. It was my husband (who has an encyclopaedic knowledge of all things Victorian) who suggested I go to see Tid Alston. Tid has a property at Oaklands Junction not far from Glenara, and her parents had been great friends of Alister and Edie. So this was the next step.

In her rambling, country garden, full of rare treasures, I did indeed find some of Alister's roses. Here was 'Glenara', called after his home, growing over two metres tall and covered, in late autumn, with semi-double vibrant pink blooms. Here was 'Restless', darkest red and wonderfully perfumed. It was one of the great survivors at Glenara but I had not known its name. Here was 'Princeps', a great red climber, and 'Mrs Harold Alston', a beautiful soft pink. Here, too, was the big rambler 'Gladsome', and the little cherry-red Floribunda 'Maud Alston' (named after Tid's mother). And here was the same little bright pink Floribunda which Mrs Murray had given me and called 'Cherub'.

Tid called it 'Suitor' and said Alister had given it to her mother, who had been particularly fond of it. This posed another problem. According to available descriptions, Tid's mother had had all of the other names correct, but nowhere in old

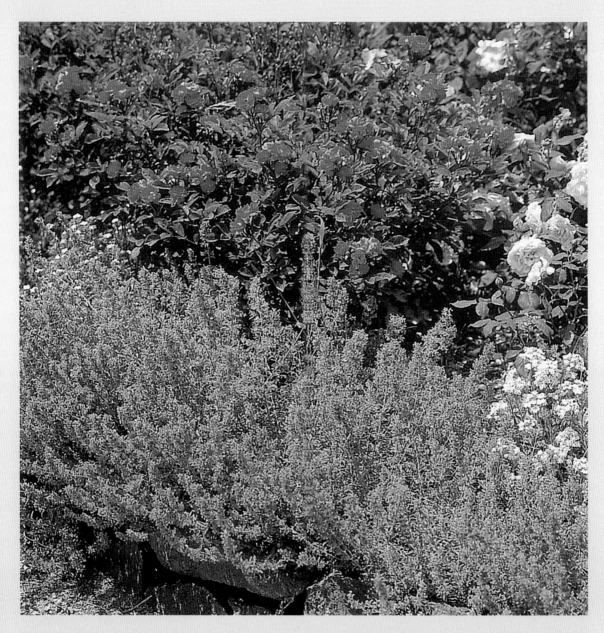

'MAUD ALSTON' BLOOMS BEHIND
'HIDCOTE' LAVENDER IN THE
ALISTER CLARK GARDEN. THERE
IS PINK VERBENA IN THE LEFT-
HAND CORNER.

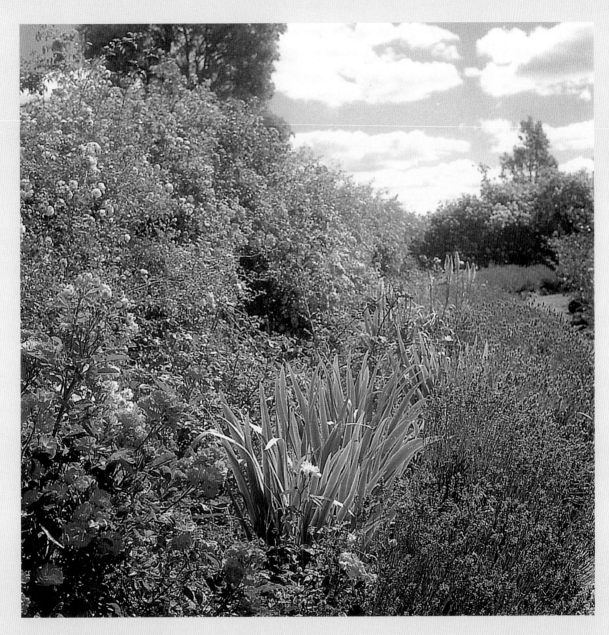

ALISTER CLARK'S 'GLADSOME'
ON THE FENCE WITH 'MAUD
ALSTON', IRIS AND 'HIDCOTE'
LAVENDER FORMING A BORDER.

nursery catalogues or *Rose Annuals* or in lists of Alister's roses had I found any mention of a rose called 'Suitor'. Perhaps Tid's mother, like Eve Murray, had been wrong? It was not until seven years later that I found, in one of Alister's articles, a brief account of it. He spoke of a little Floribunda which pleased him greatly and which he planned to release next year under the name of 'The Little Visitor' 'and another, similar, which I plan to call "Suitor"'. So Tid's mother had been right, as she had been in every other case, but Alister had, in fact, never got round to releasing it. It has become one of my favourites. Cheerful and ever-blooming, it is just right in the front of a border.

And in Tid's front garden, growing to the very top of a great oak tree, was a rose which she described as a great cream single with a perfectly wonderful scent. Alister had given it to her mother but she, Tid, had never known its name. It bloomed only once, in the early spring and, though she had tried many times, she had never succeeded in striking it from a cutting. I tried too. Without success.

Some years later, Molly Dalrymple told me of a great cream climber she had had at a farm they had owned called Red Rock. It was one of Alister's and he had called it after her aunt, Mrs Richard Turnbull.

So I set out to look for Red Rock and found it near Riddells Creek. When I mentioned the rose, the present owner said, 'Oh yes. I thought it was a briar so we cut it right down'. My heart sank. Then she added cheerfully, 'But it didn't matter. It came up stronger than ever!'

We found it at the back of the house climbing over a tank-stand. I took cuttings – without much hope, for the leaves indicated that it was a *gigantea* hybrid. I got permission to come back in November and get some bud-wood if the cuttings failed.

Early in November that year I had a phone call from Tid. 'Come down today, if you can. The big cream rose is in flower.' I jumped into the car and set out for Oaklands Junction. It was indeed in flower and a breathtaking sight. Right from the top of the oak tree the cream blooms cascaded down and the whole garden was filled with the scent. I thought of Molly Dalrymple and her cream rose, which I had also never seen in flower, called 'Mrs Richard Turnbull'. If this was it, then the one at Red Rock should be in flower too. I drove hastily back to Riddells Creek. Sure enough, the rose was covered in blooms and they were identical. I took flowers and buds and foliage back to Tid. There was no doubt. Her big cream climber was 'Mrs Richard Turnbull'.

So the search went on. Other such leads ended in failure and frustration. Sometimes – and these were exciting times – they were crowned with success.

As I became better acquainted with Alister's roses, with their scent and colour – often vivid colour, more at home under the Australian sunshine than under England's grey skies and soft mists – and their capacity to bloom again and again, I was increasingly puzzled to understand how Australian gardeners had allowed them to be lost – and in such a short space of time. Perhaps the War was partly responsible, when people's minds were turned to other things and there was little time for gardens. Perhaps it had happened because no one had any financial interest in promoting them. In his lifetime Alister had never wanted any remuneration for his roses – he gave them away, and garden clubs all over Australia were the recipients. Even before Alister's death many of his roses were hard to come by, although he himself published in every *Rose Annual* a list of seedlings bred at

Glenara. But he had no interest in exhibition roses. He bred for the garden not for the show bench and here, I think, is the reason for their becoming unobtainable. Alister himself and his friend T. A. Stewart provide the explanation in the *Rose Annual* of 1946, where Alister wrote:

> It is easy to see that we may lose Roses that are invaluable for breeding ... I am glad to see *R. gigantea* (still) in good health. I hope younger men will now get to work on its pollen and seed-bearing properties, but alas! nurserymen are shy about propagating it, no doubt owing to the small demand for it and some difficulty in its propagation.

The 'small demand' is due to the huge size of most of these climbers. They are big roses for big gardens. Most of them bloom only in the spring and gardens with limited space cannot afford them. My first plant of 'Jessie Clark' came from a garden in Camberwell where she had virtually taken over the entire garden!

T. A. Stewart in the same *Rose Annual* wrote:

> We should aim in these countries of ours (he included New Zealand) that possess so many climatic advantages at having Rose blooms every day of the year, and I know it is possible because I have proved it in my own limited sized garden. It is here that Mr Alister Clark's roses are of such value because they have been bred largely for our conditions; but it is an appalling fact that many of these cannot now be obtained because our nurserymen cannot afford to grow them. The demand for the popular varieties that will be more effective on Show Day precludes the possibility of growing many of them as the lead given by the exhibitors is reflected in our lists of Recommended Roses and is followed by the public, who demand the same varieties.

Little has changed. At the 1991 Rose Show there was one small table for old-fashioned roses (and Alister Clark does not fit into this category either), but for the most part the thousands who pushed their way into the Town Hall were eagerly writing down the names of the roses which had won first prize.

I could not now plant a garden without 'Daydream' (which Alister himself likened to a waterlily) and 'Gwen Nash' ('the most beautiful thing in decorative pinks I can hope to produce'). It is hard to go past 'Sunlit' or 'Squatter's Dream'. And still there is nothing to compare with 'Lorraine Lee' for sheer length of blooming. You would look a long way to find better border roses than 'Borderer' and 'Suitor'.

CHAPTER
24

THE NURSERY

s the boundaries of the garden were steadily extended, it became increasingly obvious that I would have to have more help. I still had Albert, but he came only one day a week. He was retired and had his own little garden and really didn't want to do any more.

In one day a week he could barely cope with the mowing. I had bought him a ride-on mower which he loved, but this is volcanic country and great mounds of stone rose up out of the lawn – 'floaters' they called them – and they made mowing a nightmare. The really big ones were not so bad – picturesque, even – but there was a multitude of smaller ones not so easily seen. Albert always assumed that if I was out of sight I was also out of earshot, and I would hear his deep resonant voice all over the garden as he shouted 'Y' bloody bastard!' when he hit yet another rock with the mower blades. No wonder he felt one day a week was enough.

It was at this point that the Fates, what my mother always referred to as 'the Boys Upstairs', sent a real treasure in the shape of Don Wild.

A couple of years earlier I had bought a dimunitive, century -old weatherboard cottage on a quarter of a hectare of land in the neighbouring village of Taradale. To my practical, business-conscious friends I described it as an investment. Privately I admitted it was bought on impulse because it was simply charming. It sat crookedly amidst gnarled old apple and plum trees, its steep roof descending low over the little front verandah, one multipaned window on each side of the front door, the whole thing dwarfed by a huge stone chimney – a cottage in a child's drawing or on an early sampler.

I renovated it with loving care – and much help from Albert – and we finished it off by planting a hedge of 'Cécile Brunner' roses right along the front fence, the tiny pink roses in scale with the cottage. We planted big, vigorous ramblers to cover an ugly, incongruous modern carport some previous owner had erected.

I couldn't bring myself to sell it, so decided to let it. The agent found a prospective tenant whose profession was described as 'artist'. This seemed in every respect appropriate, so, reluctantly, I signed the tenancy agreement. I visited him only once. He had covered the walls with larger-than-life oil paintings of grossly overweight nude women in purple, electric blue and lurid green, and in the spaces between the paintings he hung his guns, his idea of recreation being to shoot deer or wild duck.

In this alien atmosphere the 'Cécile Brunner' hedge wilted and slowly died, even the ramblers lacked vitality and the grass grew so high that the Country Fire Authority served a notice on me to clean it up as it was a fire hazard. At this point the tenant decided to move out. When the agent rang me a few weeks later to say he had a prospective purchaser I was feeling so discouraged by my sole experience as a landlady that I agreed to sell, albeit reluctantly.

Sickened by the cynicism of life in a big city and seeking tranquillity, Don Wild had decided to abandon his career and move to the country at any price. The week after he moved in, he came to see me. I had let the cottage furnished and Don wanted to buy the furniture. 'The only trouble is,' he said, 'I can't pay for it!' This proved to be not an insuperable problem. He suggested he should work at Bleak House in exchange for the furniture. 'You know,' he said, 'a day for a chair, and so on.' That seemed a perfectly reasonable arrangement and so began a long association which we both enjoyed.

Albert retired altogether soon after. I quite missed his presence in the garden – his little stiff military moustache and his shock of snow-white hair (which his wife said he rinsed regularly in lemon juice). Don took on the entire care of the lawns which, in his hands, were transformed. Edges were done with the whipper-snipper and the grass raked up and put into the huge compost bins we had built.

He scraped acquaintance with a horse trainer in Kyneton and every week he collected a couple of trucks full of stable sweepings – straw and horse manure.

He developed a talent and a love for stonework, and drove our old truck down to the quarries, bringing it back loaded with flat, moss- and lichen-covered stone. He built low stone walls so that, with the help of the mulch, we gradually lifted the level of the beds and improved the drainage.

And the little cottage at Taradale was transformed. Gone were the guns and the purple nudes. It was filled with music and, as time went by, with the scents from the cottage garden which soon extended over the entire quarter hectare. A hedge of the Rugosa rose 'Agnes' took the place of the defunct 'Cécile Brunner'. It is the only hedge of 'Agnes' I have seen. A soft, butter-yellow, she sets no hips and flowers only in spring but must surely rank as one of the loveliest of all the Rugosas.

Of course, I wanted Don for more than one day a week. And equally 'of course', I couldn't afford it. Gardens, I had discovered, eat money. And so, after a good deal of thought, but with no real 'feasibility study', I decided to open a small nursery. I had never been involved in business, nor had I any business training, but somehow the garden had to be made to contribute to its own upkeep.

I started just by propagating my own roses and opening the 'nursery' at weekends. I could not keep up with the demand. Time spent in propagating plants is time not spent in the garden. The nursery went forward and the garden slipped back.

It became increasingly apparent that I would have to buy in rose stock, especially those roses – and there are many – which are difficult to propagate from cuttings. Budding has a much higher success rate, but I had no wish to plant up hundreds of *multiflora* to use as understocks. That would take even more time from the garden. Buying wholesale opened the door to a whole new world. I met the big

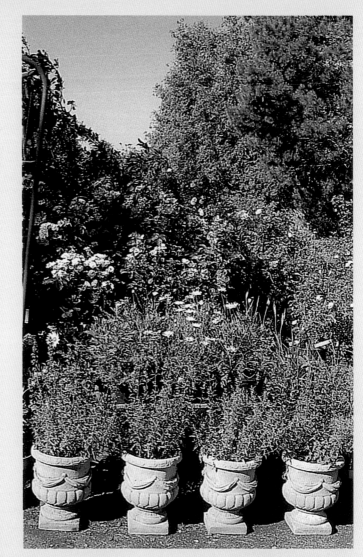

RIGHT: The Nursery
went forward.

BELOW: The Bookshop
with the stump of the
old willow and *R.
banksiae* 'Lutea' in the
background.

growers for whom rose growing was strictly a business affair. All of them were good to deal with and two, Walter Duncan in South Australia and John Nieuwesteeg at Coldstream, became real friends. John's family had been involved in growing roses in Holland, every generation of them, for over two hundred years. There was little he did not know about roses. Walter conducted his large wholesale operation from a two thousand eight hundred hectare sheep property and a grand old stone mansion north of Adelaide.

I came to look forward to June, when the big wooden crates crammed with bare-rooted roses arrived at Bleak House. Then followed a frantic few days for they all had to be sorted and labelled, orders separated from nursery stock, and all of them put into big pots filled with wet sawdust. These had then to be put in alphabetical order so that roses could be found quickly. And then, no matter what other pressing business there was, those roses had to be watered every single day. Sawdust dries out very quickly and if the rose roots are allowed to dry out there may be no evidence of trouble until the spring, when there will be no shoots. The difficulty of ensuring that this job is done reliably by often inexperienced, seasonal help must prove a real headache in big nurseries.

Often Nature takes a hand, for this is our wettest time of the year and we often had to work in sleety rain with driving winds and sometimes snow. We lived in gumboots, fur-lined caps and wet-weather gear.

Of course, things do not stay small. The demand was great and, to survive, I had to compete with other nurseries. Soon we were opening five days a week and, in the end, seven. No one wants to drive kilometres to a country nursery only to find that this is the day it is closed. If we wanted to compete with Melbourne nurseries we had to be open seven days a week. More help! More headaches! WorkCare, tax stamps, superannuation! The nursery must generate more cash flow (I was even learning the terminology!).

So I opened, in conjunction with Neil Robertson, who at that time owned the superlatively good Bookshop of Margareta Webber, a country branch dealing only in garden books. It was housed initially in Little Portion, but this rapidly became too small. When Neil sold his bookshop, and strangers took over, I decided to run mine independently. We built, with stone from the quarries, a beautiful room onto the back of Bleak House. Every care was taken to ensure that it would be in keeping with the original house. It had a high, cathedral ceiling, a huge open fireplace and every window overlooked the garden. It opened into a sunny courtyard. In no time it stocked not only books but ceramic pots, garden sculptures, cards, stationery, garden hats and aprons – anything connected with the garden.

Later the old barn was converted into tearooms. Home cooking (not mine!) and a big, cheerful, slow-combustion stove made it a welcoming place after a long drive – especially for customers picking up rose orders in the depths of winter. Its pine walls were ideal for hanging paintings. And so the Art Exhibitions started. These were a joy. They brought me into contact with fine local artists. Bleak House was ideally equipped for garden party openings on summer evenings. Molly Maddox's impressionist garden watercolours and Peggy Shaw's landscapes and paintings of the old buildings of the area were in the perfect setting.

When Jenny Phillips, that very gifted botanical artist who had drawn Little Portion some years earlier, produced her first four prints, we hung them in the tearooms. There was a pink hellebore, a green hellebore, a potato and a tomato.

These are not only works of art but are botanically accurate, even the roots being depicted in finest detail. I thought again of Dean Hole who spoke of a painting of a bunch of grapes in his potting-shed as being 'so lifelike and luscious to look upon that they might have been the identical bunch which the American artist painted for his mother with such extraordinary power that the old lady was enabled to manufacture from it three bottles and a half of most delicious wine!'

Of course, we had many visitors. And nearly all of them I enjoyed. Gardening is such an all-consuming interest that gardeners quickly establish a rapport with each other. It was not so easy with some of the bus-loads from Melbourne. These were not always gardeners. Often they were bored or lonely people simply looking for a day out. These had little understanding of Bleak House and its aims, often making a beeline for the tearooms and sitting there over scones and jam and cream until it was time for the bus to go again. Or they made a beeline for the outdoor toilet, complaining vociferously of the distance they had to walk to reach it.

One morning, when we were expecting two bus-loads, I decorated the courtyard with pots of the Centifolia rose, 'de Meaux'. It is one of my favourites. Soft pink, many-petalled and compact, as all the Centifolias are, this one is diminutive, the tiny blooms measuring scarcely more than two centimetres in diameter. With the place teeming with visitors I came round the corner in time to hear a large, indignant old woman holding forth to a listening crowd: 'Call that a rose,' she was exclaiming, 'I've got them ten times that size. If they can't do better than that, they shouldn't be in business!'

We loved the visits of the Garden Clubs and the Heritage Rose Groups, who knew what they were looking for, and the visits of the elderly citizens groups. Bleak

Bleak House from the bottom of the garden looking towards the Bookshop and the big pine.

House, being so flat, was ideal for wheelchairs and for people who needed sticks. The pleasure they got from the garden was in itself sufficient justification for the time and care that were lavished on it. We had several handicapped groups who came regularly. It was hard to tell what they got out of it, but one day we potted up some of the little Johnny-jump-ups which seeded themselves everywhere in the gravel paths and gave them to them to take home. This they certainly enjoyed.

The dogs were something of a problem. Willy hated the visitors. He clearly thought they had no right to be in his garden, and he made his feelings very plain. In the end we built a proper doghouse and a large enclosed run for him. Cara, on the other hand, loved everyone but was often too exuberant. When they produced their first litter of puppies, we put them out on the lawn in a child's playpen one Sunday afternoon and sold them all.

Perennials were added to the nursery. As I paid more attention to underplanting in the garden and got more of the combinations right, we were often asked for plants. Most perennials multiply quickly and we started potting up the excess. A splendid new perennial nursery, Lambley Perennials, opened up in the Dandenongs and we steadily added more interesting plants to the garden.

But as with the roses, so with the perennials. If we spent too much time propagating, the garden went backwards. The whole purpose of the nursery was to support the garden and that purpose would be defeated if we allowed the nursery to take precedence. Moreover, I am sure that many of our customers came just because of the garden. There are very many nurseries – too many, perhaps – and very few of them have any kind of garden, for the simple reason that the owners do not have time to manage both and the garden is abandoned as being commercially not viable.

For me, the nursery always came second to the garden. And while I enjoyed the challenge of running a business, and loved the contact with people, I grew more and more frustrated as the business left me increasingly little time for the garden.

A solution would have to be found, but for the present it eluded me.

THE STOCKYARD GARDEN

On the extreme south boundary of the property, between the boundary fence and the tearooms, was our work area. Every nursery must have one. Here were the compost bins, the old tanks for storing firewood used in the open fires, three glasshouses and a shadehouse, a potting shed, housing for the truck and bays for storing mulch and the sawdust which we stockpiled during the year in readiness for the bare-rooted roses in June. All of this had to be hidden from the garden.

So I planted a hedge of *Escallonia* 'Donard Seedling'. It grows to something over two metres high. I like its crisp, shiny, dark evergreen foliage, and the pale pink flowers are compatible with old roses. It is hardy and quick-growing.

My only regret was that, in doing this, I screened out 'Madame Grégoire Staechelin', surely one of the loveliest of all pink climbers. She completely covered a tank in the work area and made it a thing of glory in early spring. The blooms were followed by great pear-shaped hips which hung on for months. I had planted her there before I realised what an inestimable treasure she is. We picked great bunches of her to adorn the tearooms and bookshop. This invariably sold every plant we had.

With the work area screened off, we were left with an uncompromising rectangle which had been the stockyards. A century ago they had been hand-cobbled. The winters are so wet, the land so flat and the soil so heavy that the yards would otherwise have been a quagmire. But they posed a real problem for us. The cobbling was not even enough to be attractive, and every kind of noxious weed seemed to have established itself between the stones. For a brief moment I entertained the idea of a cobbled court with all kinds of rock plants growing where the weeds now grew. But sanity prevailed and I acknowledged the time and work involved and the unlikelihood of the rock plants ever finally vanquishing the weeds.

There was nothing else for it. The cobblestones had to go. We started digging them out by hand, but it was a mammoth task and in the end we had to get a bobcat to do the job. I pictured James Pennington a hundred years ago, without machinery and probably without much help, laboriously laying down the stones we were so recklessly pulling up.

LEFT: THE COBBLESTONES HAD TO GO TO MAKE THE STOCKYARD GARDEN. THE BUILDING IN THE BACKGROUND IS WILLIE AND CARA'S HOUSE.

BELOW: 'CARABELLA' BEHIND A HEDGE OF LAVENDER.

This was the only part of the garden I designed on paper. Don and I drew countless diagrams before we finally decided what to do with this very uninteresting muddy rectangle.

We had proved the value of windbreaks on these open plains and the suitability of rambling roses for making them. So the next step was to erect a frame for a rambler hedge on the north side, parallel to the escallonia hedge. We used bush poles and wire again and planted the roses 'Apple Blossom', 'Sanders' White' and the creamy-yellow climber, 'Paul's Lemon Pillar'.

The west boundary was already sheltered with a large shadehouse for nursery plants. This was covered with the yellow Banksia rose, *Rosa eglanteria* with its scented foliage, *Rosa indica major*, used as a rootstock in the early days and found now in every old cemetery where the roses have reverted to the rootstock, with the rampant *Clematis montana* entwined through them all.

On the east side, so as not to block the view across to Mount Macedon and down to the wetlands I decided on another Rugosa hedge. 'Sarah van Fleet' was my first choice. Sturdy and quick-growing, she bears her pink blooms in constant succession. She sets no hips but the prodigality of her flowering is more than adequate compensation. I always regretted that I did not plant the entire fence-line with 'Sarah van Fleet'. But the interests of the nursery dictated otherwise. It was desirable that people should see as many roses as possible in flower. And so I mixed Sarah with the soft mauve 'Delicata', the deeper pink 'Belle Poitevine' and the smaller, more delicate pink, red-stemmed 'Martin Frobisher'. 'Delicata' and 'Belle Poitevine' were fine but 'Martin Frobisher' was a mistake. He does not grow so robustly and, where he was, there always appeared to be gaps in the hedge. Here was the nursery once again to conflict with the garden.

We divided the rectangle roughly into two with a stone wall, made largely of the cobblestones, running north-south. We left two openings for rose arches to give more height to this flat area. On one of them I planted the rambler 'Francis E. Lester', for its scent and its rapid growth. On the other arch I planted 'Madame de Sancy de Parabère' and 'Sombreuil'.

'Madame de Sancy de Parabère' was the only one of the little group of Boursault roses available at the time. She is a treasure. She flowers early on thornless, reddish-brown stems. The flowers are large, soft pink and they have a strangely ragged appearance which I find delightful. There seems to be some dispute about her date, but it would be safe to say that she came to England from France sometime in the second half of the nineteenth century.

'Sombreuil' is, to me, one of the loveliest of all roses. She is an early Tea rose, and she bears very full, flat, gloriously scented white roses which deepen to cream towards the centre. She was named for Mlle Marie de Sombreuil, a heroine of the French Revolution. Gordon Edwards has a rather lurid story of her having 'followed her old father, Governor of des Invalides into the Prison de l'Abbaye and avoided the massacres there by drinking a glass of blood'. The reason this enabled her to 'escape the massacres' has always eluded me.

On the east side of the dividing stone wall, the windbreak fence to the north was planted with the single, white, rampant-growing *Rosa longicuspis* mixed with honeysuckle. I tried the marvellous evergreen *Lonicera hildebrandiana*, but it succumbed to the harsh frosts and we were reduced to the much more plebian *Lonicera japonica*. We made an alcove here, roofed over, and open only to the south. In it we put an attractive old iron seat painted dark green and, on each side of it, as a gesture to formality, an old terracotta chimney pot, planted with box clipped to a ball shape.

There were three beds in this section and I planted two of them with Spinosissimas (for which many botanists now prefer the name of Pimpinellifolias), the little Scotch Burnet roses. 'Single Cherry' is entirely delightful, having tiny, single, cherry-red flowers like small rubies. 'William III' is semi-double and a rich, deep pink, verging on maroon. 'Andrewsii' is a softer pink and 'Irish Rich Marbled', my favourite, pink and cream and semi-double. They all have grey-green, ferny foliage which turns various shades of russet in the autumn and they set small black or chocolate-brown hips.

I never succeeded in finding a plant of 'Mary Queen of Scots', but I did include the species rose *R. spinosissima* 'Altaica' (syn. *R. pimpinellifolia* 'Grandiflora'), which has large, single white blooms with golden stamens. After much deliberation I included also *R. × harisonii*, which belongs to this group botanically but not aesthetically, its yellow colour, while sunny and cheerful, being out of place among all the pinks. I toyed with the idea of putting it in the Yellow Garden, but the nursery won again and I planted it where it belonged botanically.

As a groundcover in these beds I planted the little white prostrate rose 'Snow Carpet'. Its tiny leaves matched those of the Spinosissimas as did the size of its little white double flowers, and it bloomed long after the others were finished.

In this area, too, I used one bed for the roses of the great contemporary English rosarian Peter Beales, who has given us those two invaluable books *Classic Roses* and *Twentieth Century Roses* – essential reading for any serious rosarian and for most keen gardeners.

I planted the few that were available at the time: 'Anna Pavlova', which everyone loved for its delicate pink, classic-shaped blooms and its perfectly heavenly scent. 'Norwich Castle' is too orange for my taste, but 'Royal Smile', creamy-white and strongly scented, was much admired. *Iris pumila*, pale blue, white and rich plum colour, formed an edging to this bed.

Along the east side of the dividing stone wall I planted a collection of Portland roses:

ABOVE: 'IRISH RICH MARBLED' WITH YELLOW FOXGLOVES.

BELOW: THE CLIMBING ROSE 'NEW DAWN'.

'Comte de Chambord', 'Jacques Cartier' and 'Rose du Roi à fleur pourpre' (the King in question was Louis XVIII). With their ability to flower recurrently they are ideal for small gardens. On the west side of the wall a narrow bed was filled with tulips with the creeping white thyme as a groundcover. It quickly made a dense mat and the tulips pushed through it each spring.

Two pillar roses were planted here on tripods, which I designed and got the local blacksmith to make. Painted dark green, they were unobtrusive and gave support to 'New Dawn' and 'Madame Abel Chatenay'. These gave height to this flat area and colour for months on end. *Iberis sempervirens* made an excellent groundcover. It flowers right through summer and autumn, is low-growing, so does not interfere with the roses, and is self-perpetuating as it sets seed so prolifically.

There was no lawn in this area, just rectangular beds and gravel paths and so, as another gesture to formality, I planted the little groundcover rose 'Nozomi', from Japan, as a weeping standard in a large wooden tub outside the back door of the tearooms.

And I discovered the virtues of Virginian stocks, the seeds of which can be scattered where they are to grow in autumn. By spring they have formed a mat of tiny flowers in pink, mauve and white, like the fine muslin gowns our great-grandmothers wore.

Barney Hutton came to see me and brought a plant of a white rambling rose which, he said, ought to be in my garden. Barney is a great gardener with an extensive knowledge of plants, of early Australian nurseries and of garden history. He did not know the name of the rose he brought and, when it flowered next spring, neither did I. But it grew prodigiously. It rapidly covered the north wall of the old barn and bore each spring great clusters of enchanting little white roses with the faintest tinge of pink. It resembled 'Rambling Rector' but is not identical and I continued to call it 'Barney Hutton'.

I became increasingly worried, in fact, by people's passion for attaching names to plants, often without the knowledge or experience to do so. I thought often of a story Alister Clark told of how his heart sank when people came to see him bearing a basket of roses and asking him to identify them. Were they not aware, he asked, that to date (it was 1940) over 11,000 different roses had been imported into Australia and many of them he had never seen? And how many more, I wonder, have been imported since then? Add to this that roses are notoriously promiscuous and in every large garden little seedlings crop up which are chance hybrids and have never had a name, and the task becomes often impossible. If rosarians of the calibre of Graham Stuart Thomas and Peter Beales, the gurus of the rose world, sometimes require a chromosome count before they feel prepared to speak with certainty, how can we mere mortals claim to be able to identify strange roses at a glance? There are some which are unmistakable, but there are many more which, in the absence of proof, we would do better to call by the name of the donor or of the locality where it was found.

The Stockyard Garden, as we continued to call it, was probably the most protected part of the grounds, and the individual plants there thrived. But somehow it never really pleased me – I think because I had made too many compromises between the interests of the garden and those of the nursery.

CHAPTER

26

THE ALISTER CLARK GARDEN

As the little cutting-grown Alister Clark roses in the shadehouse started to put on growth, and as their number continued to grow, I had to solve the problem of where they were to be planted.

Not only I, but also other people, had begun to be interested both in the man and in the roses he had bred. It would be a pity if they were dissipated throughout the garden. They really should be gathered together in a place of their own.

So I took another quarter hectare from the long-suffering farmer who was again leasing my land, and we started work on the Alister Clark Garden. It was situated to the north of the Yellow Garden and there was already a high fence there covered for the most part with the little pink rambler 'Dorothy Perkins', who had for a time enjoyed great popularity in this country.

About this time I had a visit from two boys in their late teens who were looking for work. I asked them what skills they had and, to my surprise, they listed the building of stone walls among them. They had never actually built one, they admitted, but they had bought a book about it and would like to try.

So with Don's help a pile of rocks was brought up from the quarries and they set to work. I did not think for one moment that we would end up with a dry-stone wall. I expected they would just pile the stone up in random fashion. I was astounded when, at the end of the first day, two or three metres of dry-stone wall were in place. It took weeks to complete but we had, in the end, one of the best stone walls I have seen. It was a real feature of the garden.

The wall was splendid, but not high enough to serve as a windbreak, so we erected a lattice fence some two metres high behind it and extended this along both east and west sides so that the quarter-hectare was completely enclosed. It was the nearest I could get to my dream of a walled garden.

I planted the Alister Clark ramblers 'Gladsome' and 'Milkmaid' on the south fence along with 'Dorothy Perkins'. On the east fence I put 'Nancy Hayward', 'Flying Colours', 'Cherub' and 'Milkmaid'. The latter is a wonderful rose – creamy-white flowers in clusters in spring and dense shiny green foliage. It grows very fast and had its part of the fence covered in no time. Fortunately I had weeded very thoroughly

ABOVE: 'THE EDNA WALLING ROSE' (LEFT) AND 'TEA RAMBLER' (RIGHT) REACH FOR THE SKY (COURTESY *YOUR GARDEN*).

RIGHT: THE ALISTER CLARK GARDEN. INSIDE THE GARDEN IS 'DAYDREAM' WITH THE SUMMERHOUSE IN THE BACKGROUND. (BARBARA STRANGE).

THE ALISTER CLARK
GARDEN

and mulched round it with thick newspaper covered with a thick layer of straw. This was fortunate indeed, for once it had grown weeding under it was an impossibility.

These were the only Clark ramblers I had ready to plant at the time so on the west fence I planted four of the superb rambler known in Victoria as 'The Edna Walling Rose'. What its real name is I do not know, but the story is that, while Edna Walling did not breed it, she had used it in many gardens that she designed. It flowers late – into December – and bears great clusters of single, cupped blooms, white with the faintest pink flush. As it ages, the blooms take on a greenish tinge. It grows very rapidly to a great height and, while it was certainly not an Alister Clark rose, it was one with great significance for Australian gardeners. On the north fence, in front of the wall, I planted a couple of 'Félicité et Perpétue' and the everblooming 'Sea Foam' – no Australian connections here!

Alister Clark's great ramblers were a glory each spring and they made this probably the loveliest part of the entire garden. We put a gate in the west fence to link it to the main garden, and one in the south fence, opening from the Yellow Garden. Over each gateway we had an arch and a plaque reading 'The Alister Clark Garden'.

Many of Alister's roses are climbers, so I planned a path with three pergolas over it leading from the west gate to the north-east corner and terminating in a very pretty hexagonal-shaped summerhouse. A group of silver birches (*Betula pendula*) and some species lilac were planted behind this, and Alister's rambler, 'Jessie Clark', was planted to grow over it. I remembered the huge mound of her in front of the winery at Glenara and I do harbour some fears that the whole summerhouse will one day collapse beneath her weight. But she looks spectacular in early spring.

Wide beds were made on each side of the path and along the entire east and south fences. We bordered them with lavender, mostly *Lavandula angustifolia*, the 'Hidcote' lavender, cut into low hedges. Both Eve Murray and John Dettman, nephew of Alister's friend Hugh Dettman, gave me some of Alister's daffodils and I was delighted to be able to plant them among his roses.

Gradually the collection grew. We had some notable visitors to the garden. From Eve I had got a vivid pink, single, bush rose which she had called 'Ella Guthrie'. One morning a delightful, white-haired, sprightly old lady of well over eighty visited us and, without any preamble, demanded to see the Alister Clark roses. I walked down with her and, as we came through the gate, she gave a cry of delight and started to run across the grass.

'That's me!' she cried. 'That's me!' Then, as she read the label saying 'Ella Guthrie' she turned to me in disgust.

'That's not Ella,' she said emphatically. 'She was my aunt and a poor, washed-out thing, like her rose. This is *me! Mary* Guthrie! Alister said it looked like a wild rose, so he called it after me, because I was always the wild one of the family.' Of course, I changed the label without delay. We had another rose correctly named and verified.

Cicely Lascelles came, also well into her eighties. She brought me a little plant of the rose named after her – a warm-pink, semi-single climber which flowers intermittently right through summer and autumn. Cicely Lascelles was a great golfer and Alister had been a foundation member of Royal Melbourne Golf Club,

ABOVE: 'EDNA WALLING' UP A
PLUM TREE.

RIGHT: 'KITTY KININMONTH'
COVERING AN ARCHWAY.

so it is very appropriate that this year, 1991, two plants of the 'Cicely Lascelles' rose have been planted in the gardens there.

A niece of Margaret Turnbull came, on a visit from New South Wales. On her return home she sent me cuttings of the rose 'Margaret Turnbull', a fragrant soft pink climber. Kitty Kininmonth's daughter came, and a niece of Jean Nicholl, who had been parlour maid at Glenara. She had many stories about Alister's kindness to all he met. In the Depression, she said, no one was ever turned away from Glenara. She had an old, faded photograph of him, taken in the garden, with a tiny bird on his wrist. I remembered an article of his I had read in the *Rose Annual* of 1945, written when he was an old man:

> One of the greatest charms in the garden is the presence of many of our native birds. I would willingly dig all day for the pleasure of having our blue wrens, scrub wrens and yellow robins watching at my feet for worms and insects. All three are great workers for our good. The yellow robin is bold and fearless and dives on anything that moves and will sit patiently within a few feet, and on a spade if laid aside for a few minutes. We have many other good workers among the native birds, with sweet notes which I cannot now hear. I leave the aphis to the birds, and they are able to keep them down ...

The photograph reminded me of a poem by the Queensland poet, David Rowbotham, writing of his father:

> You can not know the kindness of a man
> Till you see him in a garden with a spade
> And birds about his feet.

It could as well have been written of Alister. I was doubly glad that we had decided against the use of poisonous sprays.

There were memorable gardens visited in search of Alister Clark's roses. We went to the lovely garden at Delatite near Mansfield, home of the Ritchie family, one winter's day. In the rose garden – a formal rose garden with box hedges and gravel paths – was a little rose growing, not more than 30 cm tall. Sylvia Ritchie did not know its name. It had been in the garden for a very long time. It was a soft salmon-pink, she said, had a very unusual petal shape and bloomed continuously. I took cuttings and promised to let her know if, when I saw the flower, I was able to identify it. The cuttings all took and when the first little pink blooms appeared I was delighted with it, but had never seen it before.

Then one day in spring I was invited to tea by Mrs Florence Brooke, a legendary old lady of well over eighty who lived in a dark, rambling old mansion set in one of Victoria's truly historic gardens outside Daylesford – a garden famous for its fine and rare trees planted well over a century ago by Mrs Brooke's grandfather. She told me she had a whole bed of Alister Clark's rose 'Marjory Palmer', which she thought one of his best – and another little one of his down in the vegetable garden.

On the day appointed it was pouring with rain. Jennifer was with me again and said it was sheer lunacy to go to look at a garden on such a day. It was her last day in Victoria and she was sure we could find something better to do.

So I rang Mrs Brooke and murmured something about its being so wet ... not a day for a garden.

'Why not?' she demanded. 'Other people are coming. I shall expect you at three.'

It was a royal command. There was nothing for it. We put on raincoats, took gumboots and umbrellas and set out. When we arrived, we rang the bell several times before anyone came. Finally Mrs Brooke opened the door.

'I didn't think you'd come,' she said. 'It's so wet!'

We dared not look at each other but followed her down the long hall to the dining room where several other guests were assembled and the table set with a damask cloth and a fine old silver tea service and the log fire roaring in the open fireplace. We ate sandwiches and sponge cake and the rain poured down without intermission.

After tea the other guests departed but, having come all this way, I really did want to see 'Marjory Palmer' and the other little rose. Rain was no deterrent to Mrs Brooke so we all put on our wet-weather gear and set out.

It is a wonderful garden – undoubtedly one of the finest in Victoria. Giant trees form the basis of it. A tapestry hedge surrounds the circular drive with a towering oak in the centre. Aquilegias had naturalised under the trees. There were few flowers – this was not a garden for flowers – but we found the bed of 'Marjory Palmer' and I took cuttings. Then, with the rain still tumbling down, we visited the Kitchen Garden. And there was my little pink rose from Delatite in full flower.

'It's Alister Clark's "Borderer",' said Mrs Brooke. 'I've grown it for years.'

We walked down to a woodland area to see the bluebells which formed a dense carpet under the century-old trees. As we reached it the rain stopped, a mist descended and the sun came out through the mist. I do not know when I have seen anything so breathtaking.

On the way home, Jennifer, who is not given to poetic utterances, was very quiet until she said suddenly, 'Thank heavens we went. I could have gone down on my knees in that bluebell forest!'

We planted 'Borderer' in the Alister Clark Garden as a border round a circular bed with 'Marjory Palmer' and, in the centre, 'Margaret Turnbull' on a tripod.

It was not long after that, in the first days of November 1985, when the ramblers had been planted, the summerhouse and pergolas erected and the signs placed above the gates, that I was surprised one morning by a visit from Bruce Postle, one of the photographers for the *Age*. They were doing an article on Alister Clark in connection with the running of the Melbourne Cup the next Tuesday. They had heard that an Alister Clark Garden had been established, and, since Alister had had such a great love for both roses and racing and his roses were planted at Flemington Racecourse, they were interested and had sent him up to get a photograph. His face fell when I explained that, though certainly a garden had been started, none of the roses was yet more than 30 centimetres high and there was, therefore, nothing to photograph.

But Bruce had had an hour and a half's journey from Melbourne and was not to be lightly discouraged. He insisted that we go down and look at it. Even his determination wavered when he saw the neatly laid out beds, the newly painted pergolas and summerhouse but not a rose in sight.

'Do you have any Alister Clark roses anywhere else in the garden?' he asked at last, looking with interest at the west gateway and the sign over it.

'Well,' I said, 'there's a huge bush of 'Lorraine Lee', but it's on the front drive.'

Right!' he said. 'May I pick some?'

Since 'Lorraine Lee' is, at almost any time, covered in bloom I certainly had no objection, so together we picked a large bunch.

'Now, we need a ladder and some string or thin wire,' he said. The next hour was spent in painstakingly wiring the roses to the arch and trying to make them look as though they were growing there.

I remembered a story I had heard of how, one year, there had been no roses out at Flemington in time for the Melbourne Cup. In desperation the stewards had rung Alister, who had picked great armloads and wired them to the fence. History seemed to be repeating itself – at least I felt that Alister would not have disapproved of our subterfuge.

The photographs taken, Bruce stayed to lunch. As he was leaving, he asked if I wanted a tip for the Cup.

'Of course,' I replied, but with some scepticism.

'Well,' he said, 'I woke up last night from a deep sleep and sat bolt upright in bed, quite certain that No 13 had won the Cup. I caught a No 13 tram to work. There were 13 of us in the office and 13 guests for lunch, I have a hunch it's right.'

Now the draw did not take place till the following day. When it did, What a

THE SUMMERHOUSE IN THE ALISTER CLARK GARDEN WITH 'JESSIE CLARK'.

Nuisance was in barrier 13 – 13 letters in his name. And the jockey was Pat Hyland – Patrick Hyland – 13 letters again. That settled it. I put the biggest bet I've ever had on What a Nuisance.

Jennifer rang me from Queensland to ask what she should back, she having no interest in racing except on this one day of the year.

'What a Nuisance!' I said emphatically. She had never put a bet on at a TAB so when she went in to put her $20 on, she asked an old fellow in a navy singlet and sandshoes (he being, she explained later, in her view the most likely type to be an habitual punter) to make out the betting slip for her. When she took it to the counter she found he had made it out for $20 each way – $40 not $20. One look at the queue behind her settled it. She was not going back to do it again. She put on $40!

Bill had backed two other horses but, with some misgivings, and murmurings about superstition, he put a 'saver' on What a Nuisance.

When the moment came, everyone at Bleak House gathered round the radio – we had no television up there – in a state of tense excitement. Something more than dollars was at stake, and a great shout went up from all of us when What a Nuisance came home! I was ecstatic. Jennifer won a packet. Neither of Bill's horses came anywhere, so What a Nuisance was truly a 'saver' for him. There was a spirit of elation. I wanted to write to Bruce Postle.

Then we read the sequel in the *Age*. He had withdrawn $200 from his Savings Account on the way to Flemington to cover the races for the *Age*, intending to put it all on What a Nuisance. When he reached the track it suddenly seemed too risky, too improbable a story, too crazy to risk all this on a dream – and he put the $200 back in his pocket. As What a Nuisance flashed past the winning post the stewards had to restrain him from jumping out of the tower.

I still have Bruce Postle's photograph of our embryo Alister Clark Garden, but the roses have grown apace and the arches and fences are genuinely covered now by Alister's ramblers. The bush roses in the beds there flower longer than any other roses in the garden and it is for me the loveliest corner of Bleak House. Now Bruce Postle would have something worth photographing!

Gradually Australian gardeners are coming to realise what has been lost and Alister Clark's roses are winning recognition again.

A bed of Alister Clark roses has been planted at Government House in Canberra. Moonee Valley Race Club has established a memorial garden to Alister Clark planted with his own roses. The memorial garden at St Kilda Botanical Gardens is being re-established. The Kyneton Botanic Gardens have planted a bed of Alister Clark roses, and they have been planted, too, at Royal Melbourne Golf Club as well as in many private gardens.

C H A P T E R
27

THE KORDES ROSES

*T*he enthusiasm for old roses reached its peak in Australia in the early 1980s. There were, of course, a number of contributing factors, not the least of which was a widespread yearning for romance, which seems to have vanished from the daily lives of many people.

Australians are inveterate travellers. Sissinghurst had become the Mecca of Australians who had an interest in gardens. It is the very stuff of which romance is made – a poet, a castle, a moat, a priest's house, a study in a tower, mellow old brick walls – and old roses. The books of Anne Scott-James and Jane Brown became best-sellers.

Then to the overseas traveller's itinerary was added Mottisfont Abbey – a monastery, a grand old park, a walled garden – and old roses, old roses chosen by Graham Stuart Thomas himself.

We had a bad drought in the eastern states of Australia in 1982–3. Economically it was a grim time. We were in the midst of a recession. Unemployment was high. At such times many people turn to their gardens to find there peace and tranquillity and food for the spirit. The urge to create something beautiful is strong at all times, strongest, perhaps, in times of adversity.

The Heritage Rose Society was founded in Adelaide in 1978, due largely to the efforts of Trevor Nottle, who had attended the inaugural meeting of the American Heritage Rose Society in 1972. He published, in 1983, his book *Growing Old-fashioned Roses in Australia and New Zealand*. In the same year Trevor Griffiths in New Zealand published *My World of Old Roses*. Australian gardeners began to be interested. Nursery men who had previously grown only modern roses added a few old-fashioned ones to their lists. Those who had grown a few, doubled the number.

Old roses conjured up pictures of monks in monastery gardens of the Middle Ages, of Redouté painting in Paris the roses which the Empress Josephine grew at Malmaison, of the old Flemish flower paintings, of castles and English country houses – all things very remote from Australia and yet very much part of our cultural heritage, of the books we read and the history we studied.

Technology was making inroads inexorably into every aspect of our lives. In revolt against it came a wave of nostalgia, a love of all things old. Victorian houses brought huge prices at auction, antique shops sprang up in every country town, samplers and old needlework pictures quadrupled in value. For those who couldn't afford Victorian mansions, there was a vogue for 'early settlers' cottages' (which still continues). Gables and attic windows and bull-nosed verandahs took the place of the square, flat-roofed, clinical structures of the previous generation.

And coincidental with all of this came the vogue for cottage gardens. Peter Cuffley published in 1983 *Cottage Gardens in Australia* and Trevor Nottle in 1984 *The Cottage Garden Revived.* Australian garden books were still few in number, so their individual impact was considerable. Instead of planting dinner-plate dahlias and the newest colour in gladioli, people were turning to the poppies and marigolds, lupins and foxgloves of the cottage garden. And with this came a demand for shrub roses, and for single roses as opposed to the ostentatious vulgarity of some of the newer Hybrid Teas.

Membership of the Heritage Rose Society increased. But the Gallicas and Damasks, the Albas and Moss roses flower only in the spring. Most Australians have small gardens and are reluctant to give space to something which is going to flower for only a few weeks in the year. The Hybrid Teas had spoilt us in this respect and most gardeners demand roses with a longer flowering period. By the mid-1980s even the heritage rose enthusiasts, while paying lip service to the species roses, the Gallicas and Damasks, were buying for their own gardens the Noisettes, the Hybrid Musks, the early Tea roses and the Bourbons, all of which still qualify as 'old roses' but are recurrent flowering.

The Bourbons, at least under our conditions, are very prone to black spot. With the new and increasing awareness of the need to preserve the environment, gardeners are less and less willing to use toxic sprays, so the Bourbons fell gradually into disfavour, though 'Souvenir de la Malmaison' still has her devotees. The Noisettes, the Hybrid Musks and the early Teas do exceptionally well here. They have enjoyed more than a passing popularity. They are ideal in mixed plantings, and they flower prolifically for many months of the year. They have in all probability come to stay.

Meanwhile the nostalgia for things of the past, the vogue for cottage gardens (and therefore for shrub roses) and the gardeners' leaning towards things romantic had not escaped the attention of the big rose breeders. Even the names indicate this. No more 'Jet Trail' and 'Super Star'. Now we had 'Heidekönigin' (Queen of the Heath), 'Rose Romantic' and 'Märchenkönigin' (Fairytale Queen). For some time breeders had been producing modern shrub roses. Ultimately it did not matter to the home gardener whether the rose was old or new. What was of prime importance was whether it would fit in a mixed planting scheme, i.e. whether it could be treated as a shrub or was more suited, as the traditional Hybrid Teas were, to beds of roses only, and these were rapidly becoming, for many gardeners aware of overseas trends and the great gardens of England, a thing of the past.

The big German firm of Kordes has released a steady stream of roses which have found tremendous popularity here. They seem to do particularly well in our not so very different although much warmer climate, and are very much at home growing with other shrubs, perennials and groundcovers. There are many single roses among them.

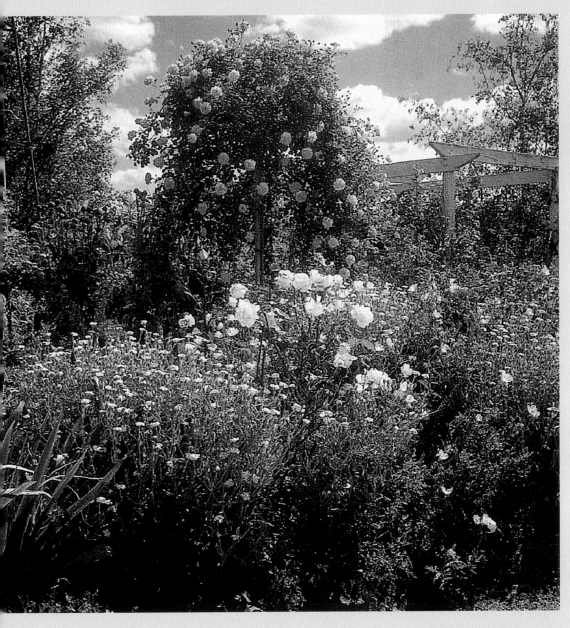

ANOTHER KORDES ROSE,
WEEPING 'HEIDEKÖNIGIN'
(QUEEN OF THE HEATH)
WITH WHITE LYCHNIS, PINK
EVENING PRIMROSE, AND
ONE VERY PERSISTENT
ORANGE ESCHSCHOLZIA.

One of the first of the Kordes roses to achieve popularity here was 'Sparries-hoop', the rose I had planted over the tank at Little Portion. Pale pink, single blooms with golden stamens are borne freely on a plant which grows to three metres. It is not fussy about the soil it grows in and will even tolerate quite a bit of shade.

The 'Frühling'-roses (Spring roses) rapidly became features in many of our gardens. 'Frühlingsgold' (Spring Gold) is truly the herald of the spring. One of the first to flower, its soft, golden single blooms come with the iris at the end of October. I love blue underplantings with yellow roses. *Penstemon heterophyllus* 'Blue Gem' grows to about twenty-five centimetres and is a gem indeed. Blue violas – low-growing and long-flowering – are ideal, as is *Veronica gentianoides*, which forms a thick mat. Don brought seedlings of love-in-the-mist (so much prettier than its botanical name, *Nigella)* from his garden in Taradale, and they quickly formed a carpet of blue under 'Frühlingsgold', the nearby apricot 'Perle d'Or' and the creamy-yellow 'Thisbe'. The seed-pods of love-in-the-mist are pretty in themselves, so I could never bear to pull the plants out as soon as I should. In consequence, we soon had a forest of blue which ultimately had to be thinned.

Quite carried away, I planted 'Frühlingsgold' and 'Frühlingsmorgen' (Spring Morning) on the north side of the windbreak fence to the Stockyard Garden. They grew to the height of the fence in a couple of years. A soft pink, single hollyhock sowed itself – with wonderful good taste – just in front of 'Frühlingsmorgen'. It would be hard to imagine a better combination.

In front of these two I planted two more recent arrivals from Kordes: 'Rose Romantic' and 'Heidesommer'. 'Rose Romantic' is a softer pink and has a smaller bloom than 'Frühlingsmorgen', but still single and much lower-growing. The flowers are borne in huge clusters and right throughout the summer and autumn. It is one of the last to stop. 'Heidesommer' is a treasure. Single, creamy-white roses in clusters cover the plant for months, and the scent is the scent of gardenias, so that weeding anywhere near it is a joy. I planted the pink and cream eschscholzia beneath it, and a white penstemon nearby.

What a good investment penstemons are! Hardy and vigorous, they flower for months on end, and when you cut them back at the end of the season you find that stems which had been lying on the ground have sent down little roots and you have a whole collection of new ones. They come in a splendid range of colours. We had a soft pink and a mauve which were wonderful with old roses, and a deep wine red.

It was Kordes, of course, who, in 1958, sent out 'Iceberg', surely the greatest triumph of any rose breeder for many a long year. And it was Kordes, too, who gave us the warm apricot shrub-climber 'Maigold', and that delightful little cherry-red 'Elmshorn' (named for their first rose nursery) which simply never knows when to stop flowering.

From Kordes, too, came 'Magenta', usually classed as a Hybrid Musk. I resisted buying it for years. Magenta is a colour I really dislike, redolent of tea-cosies, shape-less cardigans and old ladies' Sunday bonnets. But ultimately I succumbed. It is not, of course, magenta at all, but a wonderful soft, dusky mauve-pink with just a hint of brown. I planted it with 'Reine des Violettes', so aptly named Queen of the Violets, and the modern Floribunda 'Escapade', a mauve-pink and endlessly in flower.

LEFT: KORDES'S
'FRÜHLINGSMORGEN' (SPRING
MORNING).

BELOW: 'NEW DAWN' AND
'HEIDEKÖNIGIN' SPILLING DOWN
A BANK.

It is, in the main, Kordes, too, that we have to thank for the groundcover roses, which are only now beginning to make a real impact on our gardens. One of the most vigorous is 'Immensee' (known here by its German name; in England it's called 'Grouse'). Quite prostrate, it bears little clusters of palest pink single flowers and, due to its capacity for rooting as it goes along, it covers a significant area with lightning speed. Definitely not for the small garden! It has a relative, almost indistinguishable from itself, called 'Weisse Immensee' (in England, 'Partridge').

The best of them, I think, is 'Heidekönigin' (Queen of the Heath – in England 'Pheasant'). A rich apricot-pink, semi-double and scented (and very thorny), it quickly forms a low mound. It flowers recurrently, but does not take root as it goes. It can be struck from cuttings, but not as easily as many others. It looks wonderful spilling over a wall. I planted it in this way at the front of the 'Frühlingsmorgen'-'Rose Romantic' bed. In eighteen months it had covered an area two and a half by one and a half metres and completely smothered two Tea roses in its path, so that where we had previously referred to this area as the 'raised bed' it now became the '"Heidekönigin" bed'. As long as you thoroughly eliminate any perennial weeds before planting it, and then mulch it very heavily to keep the weeds down while the rose grows, its dense, shiny green, disease-resistant foliage will ultimately make weeding unnecessary – fortunate, this, since its thorns make weeding a virtual impossibility!

There are many other Kordes roses which have attained tremendous popularity here – 'Orange Triumph', 'Bonn', 'Berlin', 'Fritz Nobis', to name only a few. Small wonder that the eminent Australian rosarian, the late Dr A. S. Thomas, described Wilhelm Kordes as 'one of the greatest rose men who has ever lived, possibly the greatest rose man of all time'.

It is chiefly to Roy Rumsey in Sydney that we are indebted for bringing these roses to Australia. Sometimes, as in the case of 'Heidekönigin', which was released in Germany in 1986, they come with remarkable speed. Some take much longer. The 'Frühling'- roses were available in Europe as early as the 1940s and 1950s. They arrived here much later – perhaps fortunately, for their popularity was assured by the trend towards cottage gardens, for which they are so well suited.

And none of these, of course, though greeted warmly by the 'old rose' fraternity, are old roses – but they have the qualities we were looking for, the qualities we associate with old roses. They have the shrub form, as opposed to the stiff canes of the Hybrid Teas. They have soft colours. Many of them are single, reminding us of the little single species roses which go back to the beginning of time. And they have scent. Scent, which many of the Hybrid Teas lacked, as breeders concentrated on new colours. Scent, which to many gardeners is synonymous with the rose, and without which a rose is not a rose at all.

THE ENGLISH ROSES
OF DAVID AUSTIN

*S*cent, too, is one of the great attributes of the David Austin roses. In fact, they have all the qualities Australian gardeners were looking for at the time when they reached our market. Varying in size from those suitable for growing in a shrubby border to those more suitable for growing in tubs, ranging in colour from cream and palest pink to deepest red and rich, glowing apricot, they are nearly all recurrent and, almost without exception, strongly scented. Add to this that David Austin gave to many of his roses names taken from Chaucer and Shakespeare, and it is not hard to see why David Austin's English Roses have been such a resounding success. The names, of course, stamp them immediately as English, and therefore part of our heritage; they lend to them an aura of history and romance, evoking mental pictures of Stratford-on-Avon and Anne Hathaway's cottage, and of all that brave company who assembled together all those centuries ago to make their pilgrimage to Canterbury. So that, before we have even seen them in flower, we are ready to accept them as 'old roses in a new tradition'. Even the later names, such as 'Gertrude Jekyll' and 'Graham Thomas' link them with the greatest traditions in English gardening.

With all this in their favour, it is small wonder that they have had such an impact on Australian gardens. 'Constance Spry', one of Austin's earliest, bred in 1961, had established her position long before the others arrived, despite the fact that she blooms only in spring. Nicknamed the Tree Rose, she will grow to six metres, necessitating some form of support. In spring she is covered with large, deep pink, cupped blooms, wonderfully fragrant. I sometimes think I almost prefer the intoxication of such a dramatic performance once a year to the steady production of the recurrent bloomers. And 'Constance Spry' is tough. She will stand rough handling.

I was visiting a garden on one occasion with Walter Duncan, one of the great South Australian rose growers. 'Constance Spry' was espaliered on a three-metre-high wall, but the owner of the garden complained that she flowered only sparsely. Without a moment's hesitation, Walter seized a pruning saw and cut her to within forty-five centimetres of the ground. I must admit, I watched with my heart in my mouth, but next spring there she was, at the top of the wall again, and literally covered in flowers.

Two of the other non-recurrent roses I would always find a place for are 'Shropshire Lass' and 'Chianti'. 'Shropshire Lass' (1968) grows to over two metres, so is ideal for the back of the border, where she will produce a wealth of almost single blooms of most delicate pink. 'Chianti' (1967) is truly the colour of old wine, deepest red and wonderfully fragrant. It grows to one and a half metres high and as much across. The old Gallica rose 'Tuscany' is one of its parents and 'Chianti' assumes the same deep, purplish tones as it ages. It will put up with poor soil and some shade. I always intended to plant a clematis to grow through these two and provide autumn colour – but this was one of those good intentions I never did put into practice.

There is a great number of David Austin roses now on our market, and more coming out each year. 'Hero' remains one of my favourites – a rich, glowing apricot-pink, a lovely cupped shape and constantly in flower. I waited anxiously for 'Leander' to grow beside it. But when it came it was one of the few to disappoint me – a medium-sized flower of a rather washed-out apricot. I decided not to give it garden room. 'Hero' would have to stand alone.

'Cymbeline' must be one of David Austin's outstanding successes. In form it is very like 'Souvenir de la Malmaison', but it has no propensity to ball in the bud. The colour is similar, too, but with the slightest touch of grey. It flowers for months on end and benefits from having the long canes bent down and attached to a low stake (link stakes are ideal) when it will flower all along the stem. I do love single roses, so would not be without 'Moth' (soft, fawn-pink is the closest I can get to its strange, muted colour) and the cream 'Windrush'.

'Chaucer' and 'The Yeoman' and 'Wife of Bath' are all ideal for the small garden, or for growing in tubs, and 'Graham Thomas' must be one of the best deep yellows to have come out in recent times.

Initially I planted one large bed of David Austin roses near the maypole: 'Hero', 'The Miller', 'The Friar', 'The Squire', 'The Reeve', 'Chaucer', 'Cymbeline' and 'Chianti'. At the end of the bed was the lovely grey foliage of *Pyrus salicifolia*. As a border I used *Tanacetum haradjanii* syn. *Chrysanthemum haradjanii*. And, quite uninvited (perhaps they came with a load of mulch) came a mass of glorious poppies – softest pink, white, mauve and a deep wine colour, single and double, with the most appropriate grey-blue foliage. I could not have chosen better.

On an impulse, to demonstrate the miracles of cross-century breeding, I planted 'Tuscany' besides his offspring, 'Chianti', and then, in the corner of the bed, the pale mauve single rose, 'Lilac Charm', bred by Le Grice in 1952, and the vibrant reddish-purple 'News', the result of a cross (again by Le Grice in 1968) between 'Tuscany Superb' (1848) and 'Lilac Charm'. Roses tend to be promiscuous at the best of times, but what infinite possibilities are opened up if one can mate them across a time span of 120 years!

The David Austin roses achieved immediate popularity in Australia. It quickly became apparent to me that one bed of them at Bleak House would not suffice. So we mapped out a huge rectangular bed near the western entrance to the Alister Clark Garden in the middle of what I had once fondly hoped might be a stretch of lawn (a vain hope given our scorching January and February heat and restricted water). This bed was better prepared than any other at Bleak House. One does learn from one's mistakes. This time the perennial weeds were poisoned first. The bed was deeply dug. It had two truck-loads of manure and straw dumped on it and

was left to lie fallow for two months. Then it had a top dressing of lime and blood and bone and was left for another month.

Here we planted a rich selection of David Austin roses graded in colour from the dark red of 'Prospero' and 'The Knight' through the whole range of pinks to the cream of 'Windrush' and the rich apricots and yellows of 'Abraham Darby', 'Tamora', 'Graham Thomas' and 'Yellow Button'.

And here we had room, too, to experiment with some new underplantings. We tried an assortment of cranesbills. *Geranium × oxonianum* 'Claridge Druce', with its pink flowers veined with magenta, did well, as did the pale pink *Geranium endressii* 'Wargrave Pink', whose foliage formed a good, dense mat. The lavender-blue *Geranium pratense*, growing to about seventy-five centremetres, was ideal under the larger, more robust roses such as 'Graham Thomas' but a bit tall for some of the smaller ones. My favourite was the low-growing *Geranium sanguineum* var. *striatum*, whose flowers are palest pink. *Geranium sanguineum* itself, with its rather strident magenta flowers, I could not like, so, after a fair trial, it was banished.

We tried *Physostegia virginiana* 'Vivid'. It grew and flowered prodigiously, obviously revelling in the wonderful conditions. Soon it threatened to take over the whole bed so, reluctantly, because its spikes of lilac-pink flowers were very decorative, we removed it to a spot where it could ramp away to its heart's content. The white form, *Physostegia virginiana* 'Summer Snow' was much more manageable and bloomed for months on end, right through summer and autumn.

Under the yellow and apricot roses we tried *Euphorbia polychroma* syn. *E. epithymoides*, which formed a splendid yellow and green mound about forty centimetres tall. Its foliage is interesting in itself and we pronounced it an unqualified success.

Among the best of the campanulas we tried was *Campanula persicifolia*. Its mauve-blue flowers were perfect under pink roses such as 'The Reeve' and 'The Miller', and its foliage formed a good weed-suppressing mat. The white form, *Campanula persicifolia alba*, was very effective under the deep red 'Prospero'.

We bordered this bed with a low hedge of green lavender (*Lavandula viridis*) which has a scent reminiscent of pine leaves, fresh, when you brush against it when weeding. It was interesting but not an unqualified success. It grew quickly, so needed cutting often and it seeded prodigiously so that we were endlessly digging up and potting the seedlings because I could not bear to throw them away. *Lavandula angustifolia* 'Rosea', which we had used elsewhere, might have been preferable, although the pink is very washed-out.

In this bed, too, we planted drifts of ixias. Many of the South African bulbs are ideal for our conditions, so long as they are in the sun and the bulbs get a chance to dry out during the summer.

The cherry-red one (*Ixia campanulata* syn. *I. speciosa*) flowers very early, usually in September before any of the roses. I found a great patch of it growing on the roadside at Elphinstone near Castlemaine and brought a few bulbs home. They quickly formed quite a large clump. *Ixia maculata* with cream and yellow flowers was given me by a friend for the Yellow Garden. The most spectacular of them at Bleak House was *Ixia viridiflora* which grows taller – up to sixty centimetres and multiplies extraordinarily quickly and carries startling blue-green flowers which are wonderful companions for yellow or white roses.

I bought a couple of bulbs of the rare, palest blue one (it might be 'Elvira' but I am not sure) and planted it near the pale pink rose 'Souvenir de St Anne's'.

Behind them I put clary sage (*Salvia sclarea* var. *turkestanica*), an intriguing mixture of pale pink, white and mauve. Shortly after this combination had flowered for the first time I went to Tasmania on holidays. Motoring down from George Town where the River Tamar enters the sea, we rounded a bend in the road and came across a whole paddock of pale blue ixias. There was no garden, not even a house, yet here they were in full and glorious flower with the sea as a background. I had read that they do best in Tasmania and here was proof. While some of my others had multiplied rapidly I had really struggled with my few bulbs of this pale blue one, and still had only a modest clump to show for it.

Because it was so big, we watered this garden with sprinklers. It was a mistake. The bulbs do need to dry out and the roses are certainly less subject to black spot if the leaves stay dry. And for those with a restricted water supply, sprinklers are very wasteful.

The David Austin roses flourished. I struggled with one or two, but the fault was probably mine. They seem to cope well under Australian conditions, some growing considerably larger than the estimated sizes given in English books. Most gardeners have welcomed them with enthusiasm – some, in fact, are interested in little else. Some of the 'old rose' devotees are less convinced and tend to treat them with some reserve. Certainly, in most cases, although it is hard to pinpoint the reason, you would not mistake them for old roses. Paradoxically, though, the Heritage Rose people have welcomed the Kordes shrub roses and are now taking part zealously in the search for Alister Clark's roses, which make no claim to be 'old'.

VALE BLEAK HOUSE

ill and I were married in late 1985. He had bought a cottage in South Yarra, not far from the Melbourne Botanic Gardens, and for a time we tried to keep Bleak House going. It meant that we were too often apart. His business commitments kept him in Melbourne and although we had help at Bleak House it did not really function unless I spent most of my time there. Something had to go. And it became increasingly clear that that 'something' would have to be Bleak House.

We took careful stock of what we wanted. Although Bill's whole life is centred round the city, he did not want to live there. The years when he had owned a property deep in the forests of Dandongadale in Victoria's mountainous north-east had given him a love of fresh air and open spaces. He found life in the city claustrophobic. I could not live without a garden. We reached the conclusion that we would have to live on the outskirts of Melbourne so that he could commute to the city daily, without spending too many hours in the car, and we could have a few hectares. So we drew a circle round Melbourne with a radius which we considered to be commuting distance. The choice fell on Gisborne – forty-five minutes from Melbourne on a freeway.

So we sold the cottage in South Yarra – without regrets on either side. It had been merely a place to spend a few days when convenient. And we bought in Gisborne a delightful century-old house on just over one hectare of land, overlooking the town and dropping down to Jacksons Creek.

For a time I tried to run Bleak House from Gisborne. It did not work. I was constantly on the road, constantly tired, and had insufficient time either to set about making a new garden at Gisborne or to maintain the garden at Bleak House in the way I knew it should be done. Neither place was giving us any satisfaction.

The years at Bleak House had convinced me that making a garden is one of life's richest experiences, that it brings with it an inner peace which is not found anywhere else. But it must be done without haste. There must be time to enjoy what one is creating – time to sit on the terrace and watch the glow of the sinking sun on a summer evening; time to walk in the autumn mists; time to kneel to examine the delicate tracery on a cyclamen leaf, or watch the opening of a crocus, or a mother bird feeding her young on a spring morning. There must be time, too, for friendships with other gardeners, for visiting gardens, for exchanging plants, for enjoying the camaraderie which exists everywhere among gardeners.

The decision had to be taken. Bleak House had to go. I could not bring myself to sell it. I had a deep love for the old bluestone cottage with its sloping ceilings, massive stone walls and open fireplaces, and the atmosphere it evoked of early days in Victoria. I loved the quarries, busy once, but deserted now except for the rabbits and the birds who made their nests there – I had never made my quarry garden. I loved the wetlands with the black swans and wild duck and happy memories of rowing there on Sunday evenings as the sun went down. So we decided to lease it.

I thought of the prophetic words of the old German saying on the plaque in the courtyard:

ICH GEH' HINAUS
EIN ANDRER KOMMT HEREIN

1 SHALL GO
ANOTHER WILL COME …

They had proved to be prophetic indeed. I hoped that that 'other' might come to have a love of Bleak House and some understanding of the work and planning, the love and care, that had gone into the making of it, and that the garden might have, at least for a time, some degree of permanence.

Leaving it was hard. Very hard. But Bleak House will be with me always for I took with me all that it had taught me in the last ten years. It had given me practical lessons: how to prepare a bed, the need for windbreaks and shelters, the role of established trees, the importance of drainage and of mulch and compost, how and when and what to prune, what plants were suitable as groundcovers under roses. I left behind me a lot of mistakes. I am sure I will make more in my new garden, but they will be different ones.

All that I have learnt about roses will always be linked in my mind with Bleak House. I had developed an impatience with the long-running and sometimes vociferous antagonism between the lovers of old roses and the protagonists of the new. What is important is not whether the rose is old or new, but whether it can fill the role you have cast it for in your garden. There is a place for them all.

I would always grow old roses for their sheer spring beauty, and plant summer- and autumn-flowering perennials with them to give colour when they are gone. There is nothing to equal the Rugosas and the Spinosissimas for hedges, or the rampant old once-flowering ramblers for climbing into trees. The delicacy of colour and richness of scent of the early Teas will always assure them of a place. For prodigality of bloom it is hard to beat the Hybrid Musks, and the Noisettes will always be in demand where recurrent-flowering climbers are needed, on pergolas and summerhouses. The species roses have a special role to play at the very back of a border or where Australian native plants are grown. As shrubs in a border, the Kordes roses are unsurpassed, and the David Austin roses, with their rich literary and historical associations, their strange scents and unusual colours, are certain of a place for many a long day.

The Australian roses of Alister Clark will eventually be accorded their proper place in our gardens for their rich colours and incredible length of flowering. For me, they will always have a special significance both because of the pleasure they

THE RAMBLING HEDGES ARE
PERHAPS THE CHIEF GLORY OF
BLEAK HOUSE. LOOKING
TOWARDS THE GATEWAY FROM
THE ALISTER CLARK GARDEN.
(BARBARA STRANGE).

had given me during the search for them and because I felt I had come to know, through his diaries and letters, this gentle, fine, kindly man who bequeathed such riches to the Australian gardener.

As I turned my mind to the planning of my new garden, one thing was certain. Although I was deeply grateful for the framework of established trees there, this garden, too, would be, above all, a rose garden. No other flower has, for me, the same combination of sheer beauty with history and romance. With the rose you bring into your garden the scents and the hues and the glory of past and present centuries, of near and distant lands. They would be the very fabric of my new garden.

With the experience gleaned at Bleak House I would plant them on fences and up trees, as hedges and over arbours and summerhouses, looped along chains, prostrate as groundcovers, as shrubs in a border, as weeping standards, in tubs on a terrace. And I know that I will be rewarded each year with an exuberance of blossom, a variety of foliage, an intoxication of perfume and a wealth of colour ranging from purest white to richest purple, which makes of a garden a magic place and gives to its owner a tranquillity of spirit, a renewal of hope and a deep sense of joy.

APPENDIXES

ROSES FOR VARIOUS PURPOSES

The following lists are not intended to be exhaustive. They include simply the roses I have found most successful and most pleasing under our conditions.

ROSES FOR HEDGES

'Irish Rich Marbled' – Small pale pink blooms, ferny foliage, tiny black hips. Spring only. One of the Scotch Burnet roses.

'Pink Grootendorst' (the Carnation Rose) – Mid-pink with frilled petals, no hips. Recurrent. A Rugosa hybrid.

Rosa rugosa 'Alba' – Single white blooms, disease-free foliage, splendid hips. Recurrent.

'Sarah van Fleet' – Double pink blooms, disease-free foliage. Constantly in flower. Another Rugosa hybrid.

'Scabrosa' – Single magenta with creamy stamens, fragrant, splendid hips. Recurrent. A Rugosa hybrid.

'Stanwell Perpetual' – Softest pink, scented blooms, grey-green, ferny foliage. Very recurrent.

ROSES AS EDGES TO A BED

'Ellen Poulsen' – Small cherry-coloured double blooms. Recurrent.

'The Fairy' – Small pale pink, double blooms in clusters. Recurrent.

'Green Ice' – Tiny double white blooms, tinged green. Recurrent.

'Nozomi' – Tiny pale pink, single blooms, tiny red hips. Somewhat recurrent.

ROSES AS SHRUBS IN A BORDER

R. × *alba* 'Semi-plena' – Milk-white blooms, grey-green foliage, hips. Spring.

'Belle Story' – Soft pink, open blooms with pronounced golden stamens, fragrant. Very recurrent. A David Austin rose.

'Buff Beauty' – Clusters of soft apricot-gold roses on a spreading bush. Recurrent.

R. centifolia 'Variegata' ('Village Maid') – Palest pink blooms, striped deeper, fragrant. Spring.

'Charles de Mills' – Grand dark red, flat, quartered, strongly scented blooms. Spring.

'Complicata' – Large bright pink, single blooms on a vigorous shrub. Spring.

'Cymbeline' – Palest pink with a touch of grey. Double, fragrant blooms borne constantly through summer. A David Austin rose.

'Fantin-Latour' – Soft pink, double, deliciously fragrant blooms. Spring.

'Frühlingsgold' (Spring Gold) – Softest, creamy-yellow nearly single blooms paling to cream. Spring.

'Frühlingsmorgen' (Spring Morning) – Clear pink single blooms, paling to cream in the centre, maroon stamens. Some repeat bloom.

R. glauca – Small, single bright lilac-pink blooms, purplish stems, grey-blue foliage, hips. Spring.

'Heidesommer' (Summer on the Heath) – Small creamy-white blooms in clusters, scent of gardenias. Recurrent.

'Heritage' – Softest pink, cup-shaped blooms, richly fragrant. Produced throughout the summer. A David Austin rose.

'Hero' – Rich apricot-pink blooms, wonderfully fragrant. Produced all summer on a tall shrub. A David Austin rose.

'Ispahan' – Semi-double, light pink, fragrant. Blooms over a long period in spring.

'Königin von Dänemarck' ('Queen of Denmark') – Soft pink, double, sweetly fragrant blooms. Spring.

'Madame Hardy' – Medium sized, pure white, quartered blooms with a green 'eye'. Spring.

'Maigold' – Apricot-gold, semi-single, fragrant flowers on a large shrub-climber. Spectacular in spring. Some repeat flowering.

'Penelope' (Hybrid Musk, 1924) – Creamy-pink, semi-double, scented blooms. Good repeat flowering.

'Rosa Mundi' – Pink and white striped blooms. Spring.

'Shropshire Lass' – Palest pink, large, single, fragrant blooms with marked stamens. Spring. A David Austin rose.

R. sweginzowii – Small, single bright pink flowers, blue-green foliage, brilliant flagon-shaped hips. Spring.

'Vanity' – Bright lipstick-pink single blooms on a sprawling shrub. Throughout summer.

R. willmottiae – Grey-green, ferny foliage, small lilac-pink flowers on a tall, arching shrub. Spring.

Climbing Roses for Pergolas, Arches etc.

'Albéric Barbier' – Creamy-white, double, beautifully scented blooms. Spring. Very vigorous.

'Altissimo' – Single striking scarlet blooms. Throughout summer.

'Château de Clos Vougeot' – Deepest red, strongly scented. Recurrent.

'Desprez à fleur jaune' – Creamy yellow, strongly scented, few thorns. Continuously in flower.

'Devoniensis' (the Magnolia Rose) – Parchment colour, strongly scented. Continuously in flower. One of the very best.

'Gloire de Dijon' – Buff yellow, strongly scented. Recurrent.

'Lady Hillingdon' – Apricot-gold, strongly scented. Recurrent.

R. laevigata (the Cherokee Rose) – White single blooms, glossy dark green foliage, very thorny. Spring only.

'Lamarque' – Creamy-white, lemon-scented blooms, beautiful foliage, vigorous. Very recurrent. (See also *Roses to Ramble through Trees.*)

'Madame Alfred Carrière' – White, flushed pink, wonderfully scented. Very recurrent.

'Madame Grégoire Staechelin' – Clear pink, spectacular in spring (only), good hips.

'Meg' – Salmon-pink, single. Spring only.

'Mermaid' – Pale yellow, single, vigorous, very thorny. Recurrent.

'New Dawn' – Pale pink, fragrant, very floriferous. Continuously in flower.

'Sea Foam' – Small white double blooms in clusters, versatile. Constantly in flower.

'Sombreuil' – Creamy-white, quartered, gloriously scented. Very recurrent. One of the very best.

'Souvenir de Madame Léonie Viennot' – Coppery-pink, well scented. Recurrent.

'Zéphirine Drouhin' – Very bright pink, scented, virtually thornless. Continuous flowering.

Vigorous Rambling Roses for Windbreaks, over Tanks, Sheds, etc.

'Albertine' – Salmon-pink, deliciously scented. Early summer.

R. banksiae var. *banksiae* – Tiny white, sweetly scented blooms. Early spring.

R. banksiae 'Lutea' – Masses of tiny butter-yellow blooms. Early spring.

'The Edna Walling Rose' – Clusters of small blooms (single), palest pink fading to greenish-white. Early summer.

'Félicité et Perpétue' – Tiny pale pink buds opening white in masses. Early summer.

'Francis E. Lester' – White single blooms splashed with pink, strongly scented, bright red hips. Early summer.

'Sanders' White' – Small double white blooms in clusters, attractive dark green foliage. Early summer.

'Veilchenblau' – Deep purple semi-double blooms streaked white and borne in large clusters. Early summer.

Roses to Ramble through Trees

'Bloomfield Courage' – Masses of dark red small single blooms. Early summer.

R. brunonii (the Himalayan Musk Rose) – Small single white blooms in clusters, grey-green foliage. Spring.

'Lamarque' – Creamy-white double blooms, lemon-scented. Recurrent. (See also *Climbing Roses.*)

'Rambling Rector' – Small, semi-double, creamy-white flowers with golden stamens, fragrant. Spring.

'Tea Rambler' – Small soft pink, fragrant, double flowers. Spring.

'Wedding Day' – Small single white blooms with yellow stamens in large trusses. Early summer.

ROSES AS GROUNDCOVER

R. bracteata – Large single white, scented blooms with an abundance of golden stamens, glossy dark green foliage, very vigorous, roots as it goes. Flowers throughout summer.

'Heidekönigin' (Queen of the Heath) – Apricot-pink, fragrant, double blooms, good foliage. Throughout summer.

'Max Graf' – Bright pink single blooms. Spring. A Rugosa hybrid.

'Repandia' – Small single pale pink blooms, small hips, vigorous. Slightly recurrent.

'Snow Carpet' – Tiny, double white blooms. Recurrent.

PERENNIALS AND SELF-SEEDING ANNUALS FOR THE ROSE GARDEN

As with the lists of *Roses for Special Purposes*, these lists are in no way intended to be exhaustive. They are quite simply the plants which have given me the most satisfaction when planted in rose gardens.

Plants are listed by their botanical names, as some have no common names. When several species or hybrids are equally suitable, the genus name only is given. Common names have been added to the botanical names when they are very well known or when the common name is different from the name of the genus.

TALL

Alcea rosea syn. *Althaea rosea* (hollyhock)
Physostegia virginiana 'Summer Snow'
Salvia argentea
Salvia uliginosa (bog sage)
Tanacetum ptarmiciflorum syn. *Chrysanthemum ptarmiciflorum*

MEDIUM HEIGHT

Aurinia saxatilis syn. *Alyssum saxatile*
Anemone hupehensis (Japanese anemone)
Anthemis tinctoria 'E. C. Buxton'
Aquilegia spp. and hybrids
Borago officinalis (borage)
Campanula latiloba
Campanula persicifolia
Eschscholzia hybrids (Californian poppy)
Euphorbia polychroma syn. *E. epithymoides*
Geranium pratense
Geum 'Mrs Bradshaw'
Geum rivale 'Leonard'
Helleborus spp.
Hemerocallis spp. and hybrids (day-lily)
Lavandula spp. (lavender)
Lychnis coronaria 'Alba' (white lychnis)
Nigella damascena (love-in-the-mist)
Paeonia spp.
Penstemon 'Evelyn'
Penstemon 'White Swan'
Polemonium caeruleum
Rosmarinus officinalis (rosemary)
Ruta graveolens (rue)
Salvia sclarea (clary sage)
Salvia staminea syn. S. *transcaucasica* (white sage)
Tanacetum parthenium syn. *Chrysanthemum parthenium* (feverfew)

LOW GROWING

Ajuga reptans 'Variegata'
Alchemilla mollis
Aquilegia bertolinii
Campanula portenschlagiana
Campanula poscharskyana
Dianthus 'Beatrix'
Dianthus 'Mrs Sinkins'
Geranium himalayense
Geranium sanguineum var. *striatum*
Iberis sempervirens (candytuft)
Lobularia maritima (alyssum; sweet Alice)
Nepeta × *faassenii* (catmint)
Penstemon heterophyllus 'Blue Gem'
Primula auricula (auricula)
Primula vulgaris (English primrose)
Prunella grandiflora 'Pink Loveliness'
Prunella grandiflora 'White Loveliness'
Pulmonaria angustifolia
Pulmonaria officinalis
Pulmonaria 'Sissinghurst White'
Rosmarinus officinalis 'Prostratus' (prostrate rosemary)
Satureja montana (winter savory)
Stachys byzantina syn. *S. lanata* (lamb's ears)
Tanacetum haradjanii syn. *Chrysanthemum haradjanii*
Thymus 'Albus' (white thyme)
Thymus 'Coccineus'
Thymus 'Lars Hall'
Thymus pseudolanuginosus (woolly thyme)
Veronica gentianoides
Veronica austriaca ssp. *teucrium* syn. *Veronica teucrium*
Viola spp. and hybrids, in single colours

Iris are particularly suited to growing with roses. I have listed the ones we also grew separately.
I. ensata syn. *Iris kaempferi* (Japanese water iris)
Iris gracilipes
Iris graminea (plum tart iris)
Iris innominata
Iris pallida
Iris pumila
Iris setosa nana
Iris, tall bearded
Iris tingitana
Iris unguicularis syn. *I. stylosa*
Iris xyphium

BIBLIOGRAPHY

Thomas, Graham Stuart (1955) *The Old Shrub Roses*, Phoenix House, London.

– (1962) *Shrub Roses of Today*, Phoenix House, London.

– (1965) *Climbing Roses Old and New*, Phoenix House, London.

– *The Graham Stuart Thomas Rose Book* (1994) John Murray, London. (Revised and enlarged single-volume edition of the above three books.)

– (1994) *The Art of gardening With Roses*, Henry Holt & Co, New York.

Austin, David, (1992) *Old Roses and English Roses*, Antique Collector Club, Woodbridge, Suffolk.

Beales, Peter (1987) *Classic Roses*, Collins Harvill, London.

– (1988) *Twentieth Century Roses*, Collins Harvill, London.

Brown, Jane (1990) *Sissinghurst, Portrait of a Garden*, Weidenfeld & Nicolson, London.

Bunyard, Edward (1978) *Old Garden Roses*, Earle M. Coleman, New York. (Facsimile of 1st edition, 1936.)

Darlington, *Bishop* H.R. (1911) *Roses*, T.C. & T.E.C. Jack, Edinburgh.

Dickerson, Brent C. (1992) *The Old Rose Advisor*, Timber Press, Portland, Oregon.

– (1999) *The Old Rose Adventurer*, Timber Press, Portland, Oregon.

Edwards, Gordon (1975) *Wild and Old Garden Roses*, Readers' Union (David & Charles), Newton Abbott, U. K.

Foster-Melliar, *Rev.* A. (1910) *The Book of the Rose*, Macmillan, London.

Garnett, T.R. (1990) *Man of Roses*, Kangaroo Press, Kenthurst, N.S.W.

Gibson, Michael (1981) *Shrub Roses, Climbers and Ramblers*, Collins, London.

Griffiths, Trevor (1983) *My World of Old Roses*, Vol. I, Whitcoulls, Christchurch, N.Z.

– (1986) *My World of Old Roses*, Vol. II, Thomas Nelson, Melbourne.

Harkness, Jack (1978) *Roses*, Dent, London

Hole, *Rev.* S. Reynolds *Dean* (1869) *A Book About Roses*, William Blackwood, Edinburgh.

– (1872) *The Six of Spades*, William Blackwood, Edinburgh.

Jekyll, Gertrude (1902) *Roses For English Gardens*, Country Life, London.

Kordes, Wilhelm (1964) *Roses*, Studio Vista, London.

Le Lièvre, Audrey (1980) *Miss Willmott of Warley Place*, Faber & Faber, London.

Le Rougetel, Hazel (1988) *A Heritage of Roses*, Unwin Hyman, London.

McFarland, Horace (1936) *Roses of the World in Colour*, Cassell & Co, London.

– (1926) *The Rose in America*, The Macmillan Co, New York.

Nottle, Trevor (1983) *Growing Old-fashioned Roses in Australia and New Zealand*, Kangaroo Press, Kenthurst, N.S.W.

Paul, William (1903) *The Rose Garden*, 5th ed., Kent & Co., London.

Pemberton, *Rev. J.* (1908) *Roses, Their History, Development and Cultivation*, Longmans, London.

Phillips, R. & Rix, M. (1988) *Roses*, Pan Books, London.

Ross, Deane (1972) *Shrub Roses in Australia and New Zealand*, Rigby Ltd. Adelaide.

– (1985) *Rose Growing for Pleasure*, Lothian, Melbourne.

Scott-James, Anne (1975) *Sissinghurst, the Making of a Garden*, Michael Joseph, London.

Shepherd, Roy (1978) *The History of the Rose*, Heyden, London

Steen, Nancy (1967) *The Charm of Old Roses*, Angus & Robertson, Sydney.

Thomas, A.S. (1950) *Better Roses*, Angus & Robertson, Sydney.

– (1983) *Growing Roses: a Complete Guide to Growing & Showing Roses in Australia*, Thomas Nelson, Melbourne.

– (1988) *Botanica's Roses*, Random House, Sydney.

OTHER BOOKS

Chatto, Beth (1988) *Beth Chatto's Garden Notebook*, J.M. Dent & Sons, London.

Chivers, S. & Woloszynska, S. (1990) *The Cottage Garden*, John Murray, London.

Cuffley, Peter (1983) *Cottage Gardens in Australia*, Five Mile Press, Melbourne.

Fish, Margery (1956) *We Made a Garden*, Faber & Faber, London.

– (1980) *Ground Cover Plants*, Faber & Faber, London.

Hobhouse, Penelope (1985) *Colour in Your Garden*, Collins, London.

Jekyll, Gertrude (1982) *Colour Schemes for the Flower Garden*, Country Life, London.

Johnson, Hugh (1984) *Encyclopaedia of Trees*, Mitchell Beasley, London.

Latymer, Hugo (1990) *The Mediterranean Gardener*, Frances Lincoln, in association with The Royal Botanic Gardens, Kew, London.

Lloyd, Christopher (1985) *The Well-chosen Garden*, Michael Joseph, London.

Lyte, Charles (1989) *Frank Kingdon-Ward, The Last of the Great Plant Hunters*, John Murray, London.

Massingham, Betty (1966) *Miss Jekyll, Portrait of a Great Gardener*, David & Charles, Newton Abbott, U.K.

Mathew, Brian (1981) *Bulbs*, Collins, London.

– (1973) *Dwarf Bulbs*, Garden Book Club, London.

Nottle, Trevor (1984) *The Cottage Garden Revived*, Kangaroo Press, Kenthurst, N.S.W.

Page, Russell (1983) *The Education of a Gardener*, Collins, London.

Pescott, R.T.M. (1968) *Bulbs For Australian Gardens*, Thomas Nelson, Melbourne.

Royal Horticultural Society (1989) *The Gardeners' Encyclopaedia of Plants &* *Flowers*, ed. Christopher Brickell, Dorling Kindersley, London.

– *The New Royal Horticultural Society Dictionary of Gardening* (1992), editor-in-chief, Anthony Huxley, Macmillan, London. 4 v.

Sackville-West, Vita (1968) *Garden Book*, Michael Joseph, London.

Scott-James, Anne (1981) *The Cottage Garden*, Allen Lane, London.

Thomas, Graham Stuart (1984) *The Art of Planting*, J.M. Dent & Sons, London.

Van der Spuy, Una (1978) *Gardening With Trees*, A.H. & A.W. Reed, Sydney.

Von Arnim, Elizabeth (1899) *The Solitary Summer*, Macmillan & Co, London.

Vyvyan, C.C. (1972) *Letters From a Cornish Garden*, Michael Joseph, London.

Watts, Peter (1983) *Historic Gardens of Victoria*, O.U.P., Melbourne.

Wilkinson, Jennifer (1989) *Herbs and Flowers of the Cottage Garden*, Inkata Press, Melbourne.

– (2002) *Plants of Passion*, Hyland House, Melbourne.

INDEX

Roses and other plants in the garden at Bleak House are indexed in detail. Plants in other gardens are listed when they are relevant to Bleak House.

Page numbers in italic refer to captions of photographs.